ALL IS WELL

Life Lessons from a Preacher's Father

by

DEACON
KEVIN P. MARTIN, JR.

Skyhorse Publishing

Skyhorse Publishing books may be purchased in bulk at special discounts for sales promotion, corporate gifts, fund-raising, or educational purposes. Special editions can also be created to specifications. For details, contact the Special Sales Department, Skyhorse Publishing, 307 West 36th Street, 11th Floor, New York, NY 10018 or info@skyhorsepublishing.com.

Skyhorse® and Skyhorse Publishing® are registered trademarks of Skyhorse Publishing, Inc.®, a Delaware corporation.

Visit our website at www.skyhorsepublishing.com.

10 9 8 7 6 5 4 3 2 1

Library of Congress Cataloging-in-Publication Data is available on file.

Cover design by David Ter-Avanesyan

ISBN: 978-1-5107-7759-0
Ebook ISBN: 978-1-5107-7765-1

Printed in the United States of America

TABLE OF CONTENTS

This book is dedicated to my loving father, Kevin.

Please know that all is well, and you continue to inspire me every day.

INTRODUCTION

My father was an extraordinary man. I wish you'd had a chance to meet him, to get to know him, to have a cup of tea with him. Maybe you did.

If you did meet him, you must have been mesmerized by his gentleness, humility, and manner. You must have admired his business smarts and analytical mind, smiled and nodded at his storytelling prowess.

You might have said he was a beautiful husband, father, and grandfather—and if you did you would have been right to say it. You may have even been compelled, if you met him—as so many others were—to go out and volunteer for the organizations with which he was involved. You may have been inspired, even unto awe, when you heard him talk about his Catholic faith.

My father was an old soul, the type you don't meet every day. In his life, he touched many lives, and I doubt there is a single person out there who met him and doesn't remember him fondly and with great affection.

My dad is gone, greatly missed, and this book is my tribute to him, a way of telling the world what a good man he was. And yet, it is much more than a poignant salute. It is a glimpse into the best parts of ourselves and an opportunity for each of us to become more. It is a gift of life lessons to be shared with those we love. It is a story of inspiration and of finding purpose, and a toolkit for legacy-making.

In some ways, this recital is a bookend to *Tuesdays with Morrie*, a *New York Times* bestseller by Mitch Albom about his precious time spent with Morrie Schwartz, his former Brandeis University professor, who he knew was dying of ALS.

There are plenty of differences between that story and this one. Morrie was Jewish; my dad was Catholic. Morrie was a professor; my dad was a CPA and business owner. Morrie grew up in Brookline, Massachusetts, on the outskirts of downtown Boston. My dad grew up in South Boston, "Southie" to the chosen few of us, in the heart of the city.

But the similarities between their stories are striking. Morrie was born on December 20; my dad was born on December 21. Morrie was diagnosed with amyotrophic lateral sclerosis (ALS), better known as Lou Gehrig's Disease, during the summer of 1994. My dad was diagnosed with ALS during the summer of 2019, exactly a quarter-century later. Morrie and my dad died at age seventy-eight, both of them too young by anyone's account. And both of them were modest guys from another era. Sadly, there are not many like them left.

I want to tell you about a lifetime of conversations with my father. I want to share my observations of him, and share the father I knew and loved with those who knew him and those who didn't have a chance to. I want to offer each of us an opportunity to not only see the world a little differently, but to live in the world a little differently.

Being an only child, I spent lots of time with my dad. I learned how to be a husband by seeing him with my mom. I learned the art of my craft from working with him. Watching him pray, I learned about my faith, and was ordained a permanent deacon in the Catholic Church in 2013.

This is a book about my father and the good life well-lived.

Let me introduce you to him and, along the way, through the life lessons he gave me, help you learn something powerful about yourself. I hope, when our journey together is complete, you will have found your own, straightened path to a life where all is well.

PART ONE

The Diagnosis

L ife was good. It had been good for as long as I could remember.

Life was *so* good that I would sometimes say to my wife, Lisa, "One of these days, the shoe's gonna drop." And it did. It was bigger than I could have imagined.

And then the other shoe dropped right in front of it. *Boom!*

My father, Kevin P. Martin Sr., began to feel some muscle weakness in his left calf. Like many of us with aches and pains, he chalked it up to getting old. He'd say, "What do you want for seventy-eight?" Over time, he began to develop balance, gait, and coordination issues. The spring in his step yielded to smaller and slower movements, confidence gave way to caution, and what was one day a younger man's confident strut turned into an old man's insecure shuffle. His primary care physician suspected a herniated disk, for which he referred him to physical therapy.

But the symptoms got worse. Breathing concerns led to a stress test, which turned out to be incredibly normal.

Along the way, *more* breathing issues led to a referral to a pulmonary specialist. His bloodwork was unremarkable. The doctors ruled out Lyme disease, diabetes, a B-12 deficiency, multiple sclerosis, inclusion body myositis, and a *bunch* of other things that were even less pronounceable.

More and more symptoms emerged, and it started to become clear that something serious was not only catching up to him but was winning. My dad was getting weaker. His muscles began to twitch, rumble, and atrophy. He was losing weight at an unhealthy rate, and his breathing grew more labored. After an electromyography (EMG) and nerve conduction study, on a sunny summer day, we met with yet another Boston neurologist.

What we learned along the way, and the hard way, is that ALS is often misdiagnosed. About 10–15 percent of patients get diagnosed with ALS when they have another disease or condition. And, at other times, up to 40 percent of patients are told they have another condition when, in fact, they do have ALS.

ALS is diagnosed through clinical evaluation and by eliminating other conditions. My dad, unfortunately, got the short end of the stick on more than one occasion.

My father was always a relaxed, active, healthy-looking guy, a five-foot-ten non-smoker, medium build, topping the scales at a couple hundred pounds. Not long into his illness, he weighed in at a paltry 150, more or less . . . mostly less. He hadn't been sick for long, by then, but he looked old and incredibly fragile. He had always been my hero, my Superman, and seeing him that way made me *very* sad, and uncannily aware of how we are all *so* mortal.

Dad dragged his feet when he walked, now, and he walked very slowly. His hands were deformed and clumsy. His pants were baggy, bunched at the waist, and his sweatshirt seemed a couple of sizes—maybe more than a couple of sizes—too big. Gravity had caught up with my father's wardrobe, which had previously always transcended his age.

Finally, the doctor at Massachusetts General Hospital—known locally as MGH—tightened his lips and said, "Mr. Martin, this is very difficult news. I'm afraid you have motor neuron disease."

"What's that?" my mother, Claire, asked. She listened, but she refused to hear it.

I knew what the doctor meant. Anticipatory grief flowed through me like a river.

It had set in months earlier, and I had done far too much reading and hypothesizing along the way. Despite having braced myself, days earlier, for the certainty of his fate, an emotional numbness came over me.

"Unfortunately, Mrs. Martin," the doctor responded in a demure and apologetic manner, "it means your husband has ALS."

"Oh my God, oh my God . . . oh my God," my dad murmured in disbelief, as he clutched my mother's hand in his weakened grip.

I was certain that life would never be the same, that it would *never* be well again. It was the worst of days, it was the worst of days, it was the *worst* possible news we could have imagined.

Where was God today?

I couldn't help wondering about it. I felt lost in a way that I never thought possible, lost in a way that I had heard others describe but had never fully understood or experienced.

We were told quite bluntly and in a plain-spoken manner that there was likely no reason my dad got ALS, that there was no known cure for it, and that most people die from it within two to five years. It was a cold script that had surely been repeated many times before. For as rare as it is, every ninety minutes someone is diagnosed with ALS, and someone else passes away from it.

Aside from my mom and dad's helpless reactions, the other painful memory of the appointment was how his body crawled.

No, not *crawled* like a toddler might pull him or herself across the floor to an undetermined destination; but, rather, it crawled as in "creepy crawlers"—in that, without his shirt on, my dad looked like he was out of a low-budget horror flick with a gigantic bed of fast-moving worms under his skin.

Some neurologists refer to the crawling as "verminosis." The rapid movements are called "fasciculations," the medical term for "twitching."

We've all had an eyelid twitch. It's like that, but on a dramatic, rippling, rollercoaster scale, involving many muscle groups. The twitches are disruptions of the signals—*very* visible contractions—of the muscles. It can make for a grim sight.

A word of caution. I know what you're thinking. You just felt a twitch. Maybe it was a spasm, or a cramp.

But lots of people experience body twitching who don't have ALS. ALS is *very* rare, affecting only about two to three people per 100,000 in the US population, according to the National ALS

Registry. Twitching can result from physical exercise after lactic acid accumulates in the muscles. Stress and anxiety don't help; we've all heard of, or had, nervous tics. Too much caffeine or other stimulants can cause twitching. Dehydration, nutrient deficiencies, nicotine, and an adverse reaction to drugs are all contributors. And then there's something called Benign Fasciculation Syndrome (BFS), which is persistent muscle twitching or tingling in one or more muscles. BFS is also rare, and the exact cause is unknown. However, BFS should *not* be confused with ALS and is *not* a cause for concern. No, you probably don't have ALS.

We left MGH feeling defeated. Prayer chains, healing services, oils from famous shrines and grottos, requests to saints I had never even heard of . . . on the way to the diagnosis, we had done all these things, and they seemed to have been a big waste of time, energy, and rosaries.

I wheeled my dad out of the examination room in his portable wheelchair. And now, with different optics than I had when I entered the doctor's office, I looked around at the many neurology patients and their families in the waiting room and wondered why they were here. ALS? MS? Parkinson's? Dementia? When they looked up at me, my eyes already welled up, and then they looked at my dad, and then back at me, they begrudgingly smiled, nodded, and knew that whatever it was we didn't get good news. There was—in that instant—a fleeting, quiet moment of solidarity. While my folks were checking out, to make the next appointment, I told them I would get the car and meet them at the hospital lobby entrance.

As I entered the parking garage elevator, knowing this would be one of my only solitary moments for the rest of the day, I cried more than I could remember ever having cried. And then I cried some more.

As I started the car, "Have You Ever Seen the Rain," written by John Fogerty, came on the radio. It was Willie Nelson singing, and still brings me to tears today.

> *Someone told me long ago,*
> *There's a calm before the storm*
> *I know, it's been coming for some time.*

Everything moved so quickly. Rain was coming down on *our* sunny day.

There were no medical trials available to my dad, as his age and poor respiratory function threatened to distort the trial success rate.

Seriously? I thought when I heard that. I could not believe it. There was *nothing* they could do?

In the days that followed, my father's voice grew softer. Chewing and swallowing became a chore. He labored with his breathing so much so that he was prescribed both a cough-assist device and a BiPAP (bilevel positive airway pressure) machine to provide extra oxygen to compensate for his weakened diaphragm.

Through the years, from many intimate family parties, to many Gatsby-like work and fundraising events at our home, I would often toast, "People long for the good old days. And though we may not realize it for many years, *these* are those days for *our* family." What a lesson it was, to be able to notice those days, be aware of the present moment when living them, and have *gratitude* for them. In many ways, those days now seemed like distant memories of a bygone era, though they weren't long ago at all.

Within a week of his diagnosis, my dad resigned himself to his fate and resigned as president of the company he had founded more than fifty years earlier.

"I think I should retire," I recall my father saying to me while he was sitting on his side of my parents' bed while staring out the window into the backyard, his now-waxy-looking and shriveled hands shaking, his now-diminutive profile fragile.

And maybe *staring* isn't even the right word to describe his eyes at rest, not unblinking but reflective, maybe even afraid. "I can't do the work. I don't seem to have the concentration. My hands are bouncing around."

"You like going to work," I reminded him. "Why don't you go in and just cut back your hours?"

"It's time. I wish it hadn't happened like this, but it's time."

"Maybe it is, but how about just easing out? Take it slow."

"It's just time, I think."

"How are you going to do it? What do you want to do?"

"I started an email on my phone, but my fingers keep jumping over the keys. Take a look and finish it."

"Where's your phone?"

"On the dresser, with my wallet . . . make sure my wallet is there. I forget where I put it."

"It's there. What's your password?"

He told me and said, "I think it just needs some cleanup. Make sure you say thank you and let everyone know how much I have appreciated their loyalty"—continuing to remind me of the importance of gratitude.

"OK."

"And make sure there are no misspelled words."

"OK."

"And make sure you say that I'm still going to go to the office to say hello and help out when I can."

"OK."

And with only the edits he suggested, and with a few spelling and punctuation changes, many tears, and a subtle but agreeable nod, I hit "send" on what would now become a turning point and the beginning of his end:

> Dear Fellow Shareholders and Directors and Associates/Friends,
>
> As most of you are probably aware, I've been going through some health issues. My doctors just formally diagnosed me with ALS a couple of weeks ago—Lou Gehrig's Disease.
>
> The disease is different for every person and it's too early to know how I will be affected but it is typically one where you lose use of the muscles over a period of time but only time will tell.
>
> Since I am in the early stages, I don't know whether it is going to be fast-moving or slow-moving. It's just going to happen as it happens along the way.
>
> It is my intention to retire effective immediately and wish to have no formal schedule going forward. That said, I would like to remain helpful on special projects and on matters where you need another opinion. It is still my intention to come to the office, so I won't be a stranger.
>
> I want to thank all of you for our many years together and thank you for your loyalty to the firm.

THE DIAGNOSIS

My father died from ALS on September 10, 2019, six days after his resignation and less than a month after his formal diagnosis at MGH in Boston. He was just shy of his seventy-ninth birthday.

A Resilient Kid from Southie

Remember the movie *Good Will Hunting,* starring Matt Damon and Ben Affleck? The movie was set in South Boston, or "Southie," as it is known to us privileged locals. It seems like only yesterday to some of my cousins and friends who were among the movie's extras, and who still receive small residual checks. "Just enough for Dunkies," I'm told.

Southie is where my mother and father grew up. It's where I grew up. It's where I have aunts, uncles, and cousins from one side to the other. It *has* changed, but it still seems like most everybody there is related in one way or another.

Southie is where my mom still lives in the family home that my folks paid $26,000 for in 1969, an outrageous amount of money at the time. It's likely worth close to a hundred times that much today.

Through the years, all over the world, in New York, and in Marco Island, Florida, in Phoenix, Venice, Italy, and Cork,

Ireland, I have heard at hotel bars rousing piano sing-a-longs that included Southie's tribute song, "Southie Is My Hometown." The tune is over seventy years old, but the lyrics still hold true today as they assure you that if you're a son or daughter of South Boston, it will *nevah* forsake you. You can be gone for decades, come back, call somebody by their nickname, remind them you both grew up in the local housing project, and *still* cash in a few chips.

I have many family and friends who were born down on A Street, and raised up on B Street, or who grew up on some combination of lettered and numbered streets like D & 3rd, L & 8th, or K & 4th. The song is a reminder that there is something very special about Southie and about how it takes care of its own.

In many ways, *Good Will Hunting* put Southie on the national map. Some will tell you it was on the map decades earlier, as a result of Boston's school desegregation busing crisis, but I prefer to think people know us as the home of Will Hunting. He made a big impression.

Like Will, Southie has sometimes been misunderstood. And as it was portrayed in the movie, Southie was, historically, an Irish Catholic working-class neighborhood. It wasn't Beacon Hill, it wasn't the South End or the North End, and—boy, oh boy—it wasn't Brookline, where Morrie grew up.

Southie is different today. If you haven't visited for a while, a drive along the waterfront reveals it as almost unrecognizable. These days, it's less about its notorious history and gritty roots, including James "Whitey" Bulger and the busing crisis, than it is about the high-priced housing stock and restaurant scenes. It's less Irish and more ethnically mixed, less about long-term families than newer ones. It has fewer packies and more coffeehouses with Wi-Fi. Fewer kids hang out on the corners playing street hockey, and more kids play organized sports. Fewer guys are playing handball at the L Street Bathhouse, and more people are windsurfing at Pleasure Bay.

Many of Southie's multigenerational families have sold their two-families and triple-deckers to millennials who work in Boston and want million-dollar condos with skyline and water views. M Street Beach is now Southie Beach. The Boston Edison power plant is being converted into a massive mixed-use development. The waterfront, which for decades housed storied restaurants like Anthony's Pier 4, Jimmy's Harborside, and No Name, is now known as the Seaport District. The old landmarks have all but disappeared, to be replaced with YOTEL, SoulCycle, Lululemon, Morton's, Vertex Pharmaceuticals, and Harpoon Brewery.

"Rapid gentrification" is a phrase heard often about South Boston—but those who grew up there liked it *just* the way it was.

Some things haven't changed. Southie's best parts still reflect against the abundance of metal building frames, glass façades, and the shiny chrome bumpers of expensive cars. Kitchen chairs still serve as parking spot savers after snowstorms; Sully's still has the best hot dog; the L Street Brownies still take to the cold waters; the St. Patrick's Day Parade is still one of the premier parades in the country, despite its cancellation in 2020 and 2021 due to the pandemic. *Spuckie* still means "sub" to some of us, and *tonic* still means "soda." And most of all, Southie *still* has a very big heart. If your house burns down, if a family member gets sick, if anything bad happens at all, we have your back. Southie will throw you an old-fashioned "time"—a friendship party, which is a community bash to cheer you up and support you with a couple of bucks.

It was into this unique place that my father was born on December 21, 1940, to Thomas and Margaret Martin, both of Irish descent. His father, nicknamed Mitty, was a bar owner.

In 1952, according to newspaper clippings from the *Boston Globe*, Mitty was questioned by the FBI in connection with the infamous Great Brink's Robbery. Labeled "the crime of the century," it was the largest bank robbery in the United States to date.

The Brink's building was at the corner of Prince and Commercial Streets in the North End of Boston, the city's Little Italy, filled with old-world charm, narrow streets, the aroma of garlic, and the lost art of conversation. It wasn't far from the former Polcari's and Joe Tecce's restaurants, where my family frequently dined. The money stolen in the heist, estimated to be over thirty million in today's dollars, was never fully recovered.

In those early years after the robbery, it appears that the FBI questioned numerous local tavern and other small business owners, as they were a possible means for cash moving through the city. To this day, the robbery remains a Boston legend.

My grandfather died unexpectedly at thirty-eight after having a fatal heart attack. Unfortunately, I never met him, and my dad never talked too much about him. When he did, it was usually in the broader sense of how our cousins and other relatives were related, and how they all fit within the family tree.

My dad's mother, Margaret, whose maiden name was Tighe, was sickly. She died at forty-eight from complications of heart and lung failure. I never met Peg, as she was affectionately called. My father told many stories of her kindness, patience, wit, and doting ways. One story stands out, one he repeated many times.

"I would go to the hospital every morning before work," he would say. "And my mother would be hooked up to all these machines. She was on a big ventilator. She had a lot of heart damage from having had rheumatic fever when she was younger. And then one day, I walked in, and I was so excited that she was in her room and all the machines had been removed. I didn't know for sure, but she looked much better. She looked beautiful and peaceful and happy.

"A nurse entered. 'I'm so sorry, Kevin,' she said. 'Your mother died about ten minutes ago.'" My father was devastated, alone despite being part of a much larger family.

Perhaps that devastation wasn't only about the death of his mother at an early age. Perhaps it wasn't about the death of his father at an early age. Maybe it was about the head-on collision of many painful truths.

This was in the days before cellphones. When my father's mother died, *my* mother had just gotten the call from the hospital—but she had no way of getting hold of my dad before he made it to my grandmother's hospital room.

My father had a thorny and somewhat tricky childhood. He was loved by many people, but his family life was, at times, messy and complicated. Big families can lend themselves to bigger challenges, and a certain vulnerability sets in.

He and his brothers attended boarding school. We sometimes think of boarding schools in the context of snug and cozy chronicles, like traditional coming-of-age stories. Such halls of learning seem to offer a sense of security, a suburban retreat—an echo chamber of privilege—that promises a soft landing in life. Of course, that's not exactly true. Things are never so simple. Life is never so neat and tidy.

My father attended the now-defunct St. Joseph School for Boys in Wellesley, Massachusetts. St. Joseph's shared a campus with the all-girls Academy of the Assumption. The prestigious schools offered not only a first-rate education but a safe and stable living situation. Some of the students came from affluent Catholic families, particularly Dorothy Ruth, one of Babe Ruth's adopted daughters, who attended the Academy of the Assumption when the Babe was playing for the New York Yankees. My dad spoke of these days openly of friendships made, teachers that left some type of impression on him, sports, and missing out on certain parts of family life.

Maybe the simpler things in life were taken for granted in boarding school. There was so much structure, for example, that my father never learned how to ride a bike. I tried to teach him many times, through the years, but he never felt comfortable with it. He always struggled to find balance, clumsily getting underway, and weaving back and forth until he slammed into some hedges or a streetlight, making a spectacle of himself every time. And while simultaneously smiling, laughing, and rolling his eyes, he shrugged it off. For me it was a somber reminder of bygone, childhood days. And in those lost days, he spent a lifetime looking for simplicity whenever he could stumble upon it, only to learn that simplicity is pursued by all of us, and we just need to let it in.

Because his mom was often in and out of the hospital, upon the death of my grandfather, my dad's aunt, Cecelia Sheehy, became the court-appointed guardian for my dad and his three brothers, Tom, Jerry, and Mike. "Mrs. Sheehy," as she was called, or "Sis," to her family and closest friends, became more than a guardian. She became a guardian angel—a savior in many ways—to the Martin brothers. She raised them along with her own two sons, Edward and Paul.

My dad often told stories of how Sis nurtured and supported him and his brothers. "She helped us," he said, "find direction in our lives, and helped lay a foundation that we had an opportunity to build on." With a wide smile on his face, he fondly reminisced about big suppers, playing baseball and football, Saturday night card games, and the family sitting around the TV watching Jackie Gleason. Sis became the gentle woman, full of grace in a howling wind.

I don't know what would have become of my father if it hadn't been for Sis taking in the Martin boys.

I didn't see my father cry many times through the years, but I remember the flood of tears he shed as he prepared to deliver the eulogy for Sis at Gate of Heaven Church in South Boston. It was more than fifty years after she welcomed him with love into her home.

Our childhoods leave indelible impressions on us. Tough childhoods cause us to lean, in one of a couple of ways.

My father faced incredibly painful and challenging days as a child. He was in and out of boarding school, saw his parents die young, and entered a new family household with his brothers. I think it was through such experiences that he learned to empathize more, care more, hope more, pray more, and love more. Maybe it's how he learned to have more drive, and not give up.

Resiliency is about inner strength, recovering quickly, moving forward, maintaining a positive outlook, and keeping things in perspective. My father was resilient. I think he must have developed that quality as a kid.

When faced with early trials, some kids get on the wrong side of the tracks, and others become immeasurably stronger. A lot of them—no matter where they're from—cross those tracks and lose their way. My dad chose to become stronger.

"If your ship doesn't come in, swim out to meet it," Jonathan Winters once said. Not everybody seizes their moment. Kevin Martin did.

My dad never forgot where he came from. He came from Southie. Not only did he not forget, but when you permitted him to shout it, he did—from the rooftops.

Let's Just Be Practical

As Bostonians, we are blessed to live near Concord, Massachusetts, home to Walden Pond, made famous by the American writer Henry David Thoreau. Thoreau reminds us to simplify our lives, and in the pages of *Walden* he wrote plainly about what was on his mind: "I went to the woods because I wished to live deliberately, to front only the essential facts of life, and see if I could not learn what it had to teach, and not, when I came to die, discover that I had not lived." Imagine if we could all achieve such freedom.

My dad often said, "Let's just be practical." It was *his* call for simplicity, a way to prompt us all—whoever was there—to get the job done and do it simply.

He was deliberate in *his* thinking, and he wasn't one for overthinking things. He felt strongly that overthinking left necessary decisions unmade and led to lost opportunities.

My dad saw things as they were. He was a realist, and he was a simple and quiet mover. Those are admirable qualities, considering that most people spend much of their lives limiting themselves in the present while hoping for something better in the future.

In many ways, being practical is the other side of the resilience coin. How often have any of us said to ourselves, "I'm going to take that big trip next year when I'm in better shape," or, "I'm going to change jobs once I save another $10,000," or, "We'll do all of those great things when we retire or when the pandemic is over?" More often than we would like to admit, time passes and takes away our idealized and well-intentioned plans.

And my father saw choosing God as a practical choice, in a life filled with many other complicated and elaborate options. The loving Sisters of St. Joseph prepared him for First Communion, and taught him the rosary and how to serve Mass and Benediction in the convent chapel. Over time, choosing God was a simple choice. Choosing God offered "brass tacks" and a "where the rubber meets the road" perspective. Choosing God led to wisdom, purpose, a straightened path, hope, clarity, and an open heart.

During his final days, if he had been asked, I know my dad would not have wanted his grandchildren at his constant hospital bedside. He would have taken a very logical view of it, if he'd had a say in things.

The ICU is a complicated place, with lots of machines, tubing, lights, beeps, groans, crying, chatter, clipboards, and hand sanitizer.

My father knew what was happening. He knew his life was ending. He prepared for death all his life by living life to the fullest, and he prepared for death through tremendous awareness of what was happening.

He knew that every tight hug and good word he could be offered in his final days had been offered before, on many occasions. He knew that every chess and cribbage match had been played. He knew that every Red Sox game he would go to had been attended already, only a couple miles away.

He knew that he was in the bottom of *his* ninth. The way he saw it, the kids needed to be in school and at work, and time had to be rationed appropriately. They would already have to take some time off for the funeral and related gatherings yet to come for their Papa.

A couple of my kids, Kevin and Connor, were local, and they helped us keep vigil. My other kids, Brian and Meghan, were at Penn State, and FaceTime proved to be an invaluable communication tool.

But despite how my father would have insisted that no one needed to be at his bedside, I know he would be pleased to know that my mom, my wife, Lisa, and I were with him when he died. It's what we all want for ourselves; no one wants to die alone. And yet, many of us do, and many did during the pandemic.

But in this case, it meant that the conditions of my father's mom's death were not repeated. He walked into the hospital room after his mother had passed already, thinking that his mother was still alive. We did not repeat that drama when he left us. It's a great relief, to be able to say that, and to have been there for him and for us.

The MGH ICU medical team made an unbearable situation more bearable. For employees of a big institution, the doctors were informative, kind, and attentive. We never felt rushed with our questions. They honored my mother's request—I mean, *demand*—that my father's prognosis and treatment not be discussed in the hospital room when my father was sleeping. When we had to have those conversations, we moved to a family consultation room down the hall. My mother was certain that my dad could hear *everything*, and she wanted the room to remain as calm and soothing as possible.

The nurses rocked. They spoke to my dad with a certain endearment; "honey" and "sweetie" became comfort words. They spoke to him like he mattered, which he did, of course. I didn't realize how many hats they wore, often all at once. The nurses were the heart and soul of our MGH experience. They soothed, reassured, patted my father's leg and arm, checked vitals, and tidied up around the bed. One moment they were compassionately taking care of my dad, the next minute they were comforting my mom, and moments later they served as medical interpreters for me when the doctors left the room.

The end of my dad's life was practical and simple in so many ways—or, at least, it was unremarkable compared to what would have happened if ALS had had another few years to ransack his body. When they took him off the machines, it was all quite peaceful. He was non-responsive, his skin pale with a yellowish tint. There was no shaking, no death rally or rattle, no code blue, no gasping for breath. Instead, there was waiting, with nurses coming in and out of his room, to ask if we needed anything, a profound sense of sadness, and, in a way, *maybe* even a sigh of relief. His blood pressure slowly dropped, the twitching finally stopped, as did the heart monitor, and then, quite suddenly, there were no more breaths.

When it finally happened, his death was unmistakable. You could feel the emptiness in the room. You could see the emptiness in his body.

I had been with my father on at least two occasions when a family member died and, at the moment of death, my dad said on both occasions, "We should open the window. Sis said that it was an Irish tradition to open the nearest window when someone dies to let the soul go to Heaven." It's a tradition that I wished to honor, but unfortunately the small, rectangular hospital window was tightly locked.

Five Days Ending on Tuesday, September 10, 2019

It was only three weeks after his diagnosis, after a family dinner one warm Thursday, on the most uneventful of late summer evenings, and with no warning, that my dad aspirated and wound up in the ICU of one of the world's best hospitals.

Intubation is the process of inserting an endotracheal tube through the mouth and into the airway. This is done to help get air in and out of the patient's lungs. My father was intubated upon being admitted to the ER. When he was awake, he had no way to communicate with us, so he began writing notes with a thin black Sharpie in a journal provided by MGH. His writing style was distinct in many ways, more Calibri font than Times New Roman: readable, with clean lines, and aesthetically pleasing. It got the job done without fanfare, even now.

Looking back, the journal not only became the record of his hospital stay but the record of his death and of the final days of his life. It has become *the* most precious gift he ever gave us. When I call my mom and ask what she is doing, it is not uncommon for her to say, "I'm just looking through your father's hospital journal."

Some of the notes were rudimentary, like asking what time it was or what type of medicine he was receiving. Others made it clear that he wanted to be engaged in his treatment program; he wrote, "I want to know everything," or, "Have Lisa come in each time so we make sure we're all on the same page." The most difficult notes, written with his IV-bruised, unsteady hand, spoke to the end of his life. They hinted that he knew *more* about what was going on than we did, that he knew the end was nearer than any of us understood.

He wrote, "You have to realize that each day is a struggle to live."

We slept in shifts at my dad's hospital bedside and in the ICU waiting room. It's astonishing how comfortable those stackable steel frame chairs and a blanket can be when you need a brief rest out of sheer exhaustion. What's more notable is the endless array of setup possibilities they offer.

I had never been more tired. Not that we were looking for some, but there was no downtime. Somehow, hours felt like an eternity, and yet days passed in a rapid haze. My back was sore from sitting. My back was sore from standing. And my back was sore from leaning against the wall. Little things became big things, like arranging tissues and papers and pens and iPhones and chargers on the rolling tray table.

The room was as devoid of beauty as I was devoid of hope. Going to the hospital cafeteria became an elaborate outing, creating the opportunity not only to eat but to escape from the reality of it all, maybe a chance to sneak outside and breathe some fresh air, maybe a chance to listen. One of the hardest—yet simplest—things to do in life is to listen.

Hospitals are not easy on the senses. Not all the smells are good, and some are quite offensive. Soaps, bleach, antiseptics, and bodily fluids all overlap in an overpowering way. The ICU brings together the hubbub of patients crying out in pain, families comforting one another from bad news, loud TVs hanging from the ceiling, and hospital staff busily doing their jobs. The rooms were typical . . . sparse, impersonal, and functional. It was unclear if the chair rail was supposed to be a decorative feature or a protective barrier from wheelchairs and hospital beds. It seemed to accomplish neither.

Although the ICU didn't formally allow sleepovers, visitors were permitted at any time, and no one was more steadfast than my mom. As I look back, I think how fortunate we were to be able to be with my dad in the hospital, unlike so many other families who were separated from their sick loved ones during the pandemic. I still don't know how my mom did it, but what I do know is that at *every* moment, and in *every* decision, she exemplified her own resilience, care, grace, and unwavering protection of and love for my dad. In so many ways, she continued the conversation about what matters most, what it means to be a family, and *why* it matters to be a family. Despite the plot twist in her own life, she continued to plant seeds for all of us. It, too, was a lesson.

Like so many of us who have been in similar shoes, we prayed for a hospital miracle, a Hail Mary pass from God. I'm a Catholic permanent deacon, ordained in 2013 by Boston's Cardinal Archbishop Sean O'Malley, with a strong faith bestowed upon me by my parents.

I had been struggling with my faith for months. I felt separated from God, empty, and emotionally exhausted. It felt dark, the type of dark that comes long before the sunrise, the type of dark that robs you of peace and life's pleasure and paralyzes you with worry and anxiety. The type of dark that causes night sweats and soaked sheets.

For some reason, God didn't seem to be listening. I felt liable, particularly given that, as a deacon, I saw myself as some sort of poster child for what Catholics believe. God's love has many faces, but this did not seem like one of them.

How many times have I walked into similar hospital rooms, "selling the Creed" of what we believe, to families desperately looking for hope? Many, many times.

We all stumble, and I had tripped in a very big way. Forgive me, friends, for I have sinned. It is humbling to make this confession to you.

Deacons can be a confusing bunch. There are currently about 17,000 Catholic permanent deacons in the United States. We are not priests, but we are ordained ministers. We are clergy, which means we are not laypeople. We can wear "the collar" when we are representing the church, but we wear business attire in the community. We can preach, baptize, officiate at a Catholic wedding, bury the dead, and in some dioceses can even run a parish. Permanent deacons are often married but can't get married again if their spouse dies—and so deacons work *really* hard to keep their wives healthy.

Deacons are called to represent the church in the community. We are called to embody Christ as a servant to others and to take up social justice causes such as affordable housing, poverty, and immigration. Mostly, deacons are the "hug of the church" to the poor, marginalized, and all those living in the shadows of society.

Deacons are called to the ministry of love. My ordination prayer card contains the words of "Fall in Love," a prayer attributed to Fr. Pedro Arrupe, SJ (1907–1991).

> *Nothing is more practical than finding God,*
> *than falling in Love in quite an absolute, final way.*
> *What you are in love with, what seizes your imagination,*
> *will affect everything. It will decide what will get you out*
> *of bed in the morning, what you do with your evenings,*
> *how you spend your weekends, what you read, whom you know,*
> *what breaks your heart, and what amazes you with joy and*
> *gratitude. Fall in Love, stay in Love, and it will decide everything.*

Before he lost the use of his legs, before he could no longer raise his arms for an embrace, before he could no longer speak, to be the peacemaker or provide words of comfort, my dad died in the most ordinary of ways. Sometimes mustard seed faith will do: even a small amount can be enough. And, at that exact moment, that's what I had. Sometimes things are only real if you choose to believe in them. And through an aperture to the Beatitudes, we trusted that God offered mercy to a man who had been merciful to *many* more.

——————

It was 11:26 a.m. on Tuesday, September 10, 2019, when my father passed away, five days after entering MGH. He was pronounced dead at 11:37 a.m. by the attending physician. Apparently, you're not dead until the doctor says you are.

As the heart monitor flatlined, I stared at my lifeless dad, lying in the hospital bed. And when I looked at my mom, heartbroken and exhausted, she was clutching his hand, her head against his side.

I saw the breath go out of her.

Is Anybody Listening?

"What do we do now?" I can remember my Aunt Eileen asking, in a hospital room many years earlier. Her husband, Tom, had just died. He was my uncle, my father's brother. My dad opened the hospital room window to let Tom's soul depart. And on the day my father died, we asked the same question. "What do we do now?"

I guess we were supposed to get into the car, roll down the windows, and use some type of hospital-provided bullhorn to announce my father's passing as we drove to my mother's house, twenty minutes away.

The world, of course, would stop once it learned the news. Or, at least, all of Boston would shut down and mourn along with us.

Instead, there was no PA announcement or newsflash, and nothing around us stopped, not even the meter at the hospital garage where we had parked five days earlier. If you have not yet experienced it, you will: the earth doesn't stop rotating for your grief.

Rather than go back to my parents' house, or to my own, and find an onslaught of family and friends expressing their condolences with hugs, belabored conversation, sandwich platters, and trays of homemade pasta and chicken parmigiana, we chose an unconventional—but practical—path and opted to stay at The Liberty Hotel, a former Boston jail, next to MGH, and use it as basecamp and place of refuge while we made the obligatory calls about my dad's passing. We used it as a gathering place for the kids, ate comfort food, and tried to get some needed sleep, which we had not had for five days.

My father died quietly and with dignity. He died surrounded by love. He died holding hands with my mother, something they had done *every* night when they had gone to bed for decades. The sterile, hand sanitizer aroma of his hospital room gave way to the sweet smell of roses. And although Boston didn't stop the day my father died, it did take notice.

Anger, despair, sadness, hurt . . . they all reared their ugly heads within a few short hours. We didn't get the miracle of new life. Lazarus wasn't raised from the dead this time. I *so* wanted that.

Jesus cries when his friend, Lazarus, dies. He is moved to tears because He sees the power that death has over the living. He sees how death affects their relationship with Him. Death is the greatest threat to our faith. And, knowing this, Jesus reminds us from the onset when He says, "This illness is not to end in death, but is for the glory of God, that the Son of God may be glorified through it." (John 11:4) Jesus affirms that we will not be conquered by death. He calls us forth to something more, something purposeful, and something hopeful.

We *did* get a miracle. It was a different kind of miracle, with many moments of grace. We got the miracle of a peaceful death and the promise of eternal life.

My father trusted in God's timing; why shouldn't I?

———————

Miracles are a funny thing, aren't they? Everyone deserves one. The father with colon cancer. The elderly mom going in for brain surgery. The victim of a bad car accident. The COVID patient who got sick while shopping for their family's groceries. Aunt Theresa. Cousin Bill. The unemployed factory worker who's enduring a home foreclosure.

I don't mean to sound harsh, but maybe *none* of us deserves a miracle.

I wonder if our expectations are too high. I wonder if that's why so many people frequently seem mad at God. *Maybe* that's the reason why *I* found myself angry, frustrated, and discouraged—because somehow, I thought, my dad deserved a little help behind the scenes.

That's another tough one to admit. I do believe that God intervenes at times, that He is working in the background, and that He is preparing the way. I don't believe He intervenes because people somehow deserve a miracle. None of us has earned the right to be saved more than another. There must be a larger purpose to how the stars align, and we will *never* understand what that larger purpose might be.

In one of its *many* definitions, faith is about believing in God even when He chooses *not* to step in. Especially today, at the tail-end of a worldwide pandemic, doesn't that give us pause?

Miracles are a mystery. When and how does God swoop in to save us at *precisely* the opportune moment?

Remember that time you stepped off the curb and stepped back *just* in time. Was that God? And if it was, do we immediately fall back to our old ways and do nothing to heal our lives?

I see miracles as an occurrence, or a series of occurrences, that happen in the blind spot of our lives. The illusionist wants us to look *here*, while something is happening *there*. Perhaps it is *there* where we should be focused. Perhaps *there* is where God is searching for us. Perhaps *there* is where we can find Him.

For instance, take the family members who have been distant for many years because of the nasty breakup of the family business. Dad dies years later, and the family uses that moment as the inflection point to double down on the importance of their family relationships going forward. The family prayed for the bedside miracle, and ironically, the miracle received is the family reengaging in what matters most.

I wonder if it makes sense, at least sometimes, to let God give us what we *need* rather than what we *want*? And in doing so, when we wander, we not only let God search for us, we let Him find us.

After a rough childhood, maybe my dad getting on the right path was a miracle. Maybe meeting my mom when they were both thirteen was a miracle. Maybe the beautiful marriage they shared was a miracle. Maybe not getting diagnosed with ALS until he was seventy-eight and dying less than a month later was a miracle.

Sure, I'm still thinking about that one. Meditate often, pray more, and be attentive to the illusionist in your life and where they want you to look. Reframe the picture in your mind.

A few days before he died, one of my dad's hospital notes read, "It's the end . . . been to Heaven." Later, when the tube had been taken out of his throat, he told us in a raspy voice that he had seen a beautiful altar, white with gold, adorned with sweet-smelling flowers and angels and candles. He said that the Holy Family had come out to meet him, that they had given him a hug, and that Mary had whispered in his ear. Mary said the family would see him again on Tuesday and that *all would be well again.*

The Funeral

We didn't have a wake for my father at the local funeral parlor. We held it someplace more familiar, a place we knew he cherished, a place he loved, an offering to our family from the pastor my mom and dad appreciated so much.

He was waked out of the church he helped to save more than a decade earlier. His casket sat to the left of the stained-glass window that bears our family's name.

In 2004, Gate of Heaven Church was slated to close, as part of Cardinal O'Malley's plan to close or consolidate a number of the 357 churches in the Archdiocese of Boston, citing low Mass attendance, a shortage of priests, and financial constraints that resulted from the clergy abuse crisis.

Back in the day, the Catholic Church was the center of community life in neighborhoods like Southie. The church offered, among many other things, St. Patrick's Day dinner dances, Bible study, picnics, CYO basketball, Christmas bazaars and, of course, church bingo, complete with fluorescent lighting. The parish community was so synonymous with the neighborhood that residents talked always in terms of what parish they were from, and not what street they lived on. But those days, for the most part, have unfortunately been gone for decades only to be replaced with parish mergers, clusters, and closures.

My father had become an important part of the Gate of Heaven leadership team. He tremendously admired, respected, and became a close confidante and friend to the pastor, Reverend Robert E. Casey. Through the years, my father had been chair of the parish and finance councils, and had sat on many *ad hoc* committees. But nothing brought him more personal reward than being an Extraordinary Minister of Holy Communion, being the bearer of the body of Christ to the faithful.

While they were eating, Jesus took bread, said the blessing, broke it, and giving it to his disciples, said, "Take and eat; this is my body." Then he took a cup, gave thanks, and gave it to them, saying, "Drink from it, all of you, for this is my blood of the covenant, which will be shed on behalf of many for the forgiveness of sins." (Matthew 26: 26-28)

Catholics believe that Jesus is really and substantially present in the Eucharist, not metaphorically or symbolically. We believe what He said. This *is* my body. That meant my father carried Christ's own flesh to fellow members of his community; that he was entrusted with a reverent and sacred role. What's *not* to like about that? My dad was a holy deliveryman!

Established in 1863, Gate of Heaven required more than $6 million in renovations, to restore it to its former glory.

1863—a long time ago.

"How long ago was it?" Johnny Carson may have asked his audience.

It was the year Abraham Lincoln delivered the Gettysburg Address. It was the year of the Emancipation Proclamation, a year when the country was in flux and no one knew if the union would survive or if slaves would really be made free. Gate of Heaven had seen a great deal of history. It had stood through world wars and the Great Depression, among many other things.

My father had made all his sacraments at Gatey, as it was warmly called by locals. He and many others were unwavering in their love for the place and their desire to preserve it.

Gatey was one of the largest churches in Boston. It could offer the city a vibrant and dynamic worship center and campus. Dad figured that if the Catholic Church were to go through another consolidation, fifty or 100 years down the road, if the church was different in ways that we could not yet imagine, Gatey could play a role the likes of which nobody could anticipate.

The archdiocese agreed to keep the church open if the parish could raise the necessary funds. My dad led the capital campaign, and my parents came out of the gate making the lead gift. The work included cleaning, pointing, and rebuilding masonry; replacement of copper flashings and gutters; restoration of stained-glass windows; structural repair of the spire; new mechanical and electrical systems; and a vibrant repainting of the interior to its original colors.

The church received Preservation Awards, in 2007, from the Boston Preservation Alliance and Massachusetts Historical Commission. Today, the Gate of Heaven steeple, a beacon of hope for so many, which can be seen across Boston and far beyond, is named after the "Kevin and Claire Martin Family." My kids and their kids will be able to retell this beautiful story of their Nina and Papa's generosity for generations to come, and I am incredibly proud of that.

Over 1,000 people filed through Dad's wake receiving line at Gatey, many of whom seem a blur to me now. Funny, I can't tell you who was there, but my mom and I can tell you who wasn't. Grief does that.

I was told that, at times, the line was over two hours long. While they waited, many people got to know their new, compulsory neighbors, and told stories about my father. They told me variations of the same story: "Your father was the kindest, most giving, unassuming person I knew." They recounted tales of his kindness, good works, empathy, and comfort; his care for the hungry and the homeless; and his leadership in saving his parish church and doing so much more for the South Boston community. They told stories of how smart he was and how he brought value to their businesses. They told stories about how he had inspired them "to do more and to do better" by his faith example.

One not-for-profit executive director told me that my father had anonymously donated funds to his organization for a new playground, and that my dad had insisted on no recognition, but that once it was completed, he wanted to come by with my mom to see the kids at play. And they did.

A case worker from a substance abuse center told me that every year, a few days before Christmas, my father would stop by with a large manila envelope containing all sorts of gift cards to be disbursed to the residents. He said Kevin would make no big deal of it, always commenting, "It's just enough that the guys can get some underwear, socks, toiletries, practical things like that."

My father was a holy man. He believed that prayer brought us closer to God.

I can remember him reading the Bible in bed. It was what he did to calm and settle his mind from the long day. Growing up, he told me stories about Old Testament prophets like Amos, Daniel, Jeremiah, Micah, and Isaiah.

My dad fell in love and stayed in love with my mom, his family, and his God. That is what got him out of bed in the morning. And even though he wasn't feeling well for close to a year, he lived each day to its fullest. He was a man who spent his entire life helping others in large and small ways. He was addicted to the good in humanity for everything pure and right.

The Mass of a Christian Burial was flawless. Hundreds and hundreds of mourners came together on the most perfect of late summer days. The single bagpiper was a reminder of our Irish roots. More than one would not have been practical, could have even been downright flaunty, according to my mom.

A dozen priests and deacons greeted us, including the local bishop, who informed the mourners that Cardinal Sean would have been in attendance, were it not for a meeting with Pope Francis at the Vatican. The cardinal had, he said, offered Mass that morning for my father in Rome.

I was humbled and privileged to offer the homily at his funeral. At first, as an only child, I didn't want to be separated from my mom sitting in that first pew—but, after reflection, I knew that she would be with my wife and kids, and nobody could better offer the homily for the father of a permanent deacon than the deacon himself. *And nobody could share the life lessons taught by a preacher's father better than his only son.*

As much as I thought I would, I didn't break down. On several occasions, I paused for emphasis, but those pauses also allowed me brief moments to regain my composure. He was my dad, but I had a job to do, and I took that job seriously. I looked out, felt a twitch in my right calf, and gently smiled.

"My Dear Brothers and Sisters in Christ," I began slowly.

"Good morning, and thank you," I offered as I nodded my head and looked to my mother and family as if I were somehow seeking permission to begin.

> On behalf of my mother, Claire, and my wife, Lisa, and our kids—Kevin, Connor, Brian, and Meghan—I want to thank you all for coming out this morning to honor my dad. He would be so incredibly touched by this outpouring of love and affection. Thank you . . . Bishop Hennessey, Fr. Casey . . . and to so many of my dear priest and deacon friends for being here today. And thank you to the sixth-grade class of the South Boston Catholic Academy for being here—you are our future, and because of you, that future looks so incredibly bright.

I did not realize until the previous evening that the students would be in attendance. It was touching, and I was moved as I looked out at their innocent faces, and I could not help but wonder what they really understood about what was taking place at that moment. I went on:

> Without a doubt, this moment is surreal. My dad was a superhero—many of you know that—and he was my superhero . . . and as crazy as it sounds, I somehow thought that my dad was going to live forever . . . or at least for a very, very long time.
>
> Now admit it. All of us Google some crazy stuff . . . that moment when we escape from reality—even if just for a few minutes. And so . . . if you Google, "What are the odds . . . " so many unusual things come up . . . things that mostly don't matter . . . but things that are at least engrossing for a few brief moments.
>
> Did you know that:
> - The odds of having twins are one out of 250.
> - The odds of getting a hole in one is one in 6,000.
> - The lifetime odds of being struck by lightning is one in 4,000.
> - The odds of being audited by the IRS is one in 200; my dad would want you to know that.
> - And . . . the odds of being diagnosed with ALS is about two to three out of 100,000. It's a very rare disease.

I wanted people to know that my dad had died from ALS. Maybe it would cause them to take action or to make a donation to The ALS Association, as requested in the obituary.

Over the course of ten to twelve minutes, I offered reflections about my father and about what he taught us, and about what lessons he offered me. That homily, in many ways, became the basis for this book, and I am happy to share the entirety of it with you in the Epilogue.

Although I was speaking as a son, I was also speaking as a deacon, and I tried to adhere to many of the rubrics learned in my homiletics class in the seminary: don't make it a eulogy, that is not the point. Don't canonize the deceased, only God can do that. We are "practicing Catholics" for a reason; none of us has perfected it. Provide some amount of catechesis, the people in the pews are starving for it.

I recall the funeral homily of associate Justice of the Supreme Court, Antonin Scalia, given by his son, Fr. Paul Scalia. He started it *exceptionally* when he said, "We are gathered here because of one man. A man known personally to many of us, known only by reputation to even more. A man loved by many, scorned by others. A man known for great controversy, and for great compassion. That man, of course, is Jesus of Nazareth." A good homily, especially a funeral homily, is born out of love, hard work, and prayer.

I got an applause for the homily. In fact, the second half of the church gave it a standing ovation; the very front of the church didn't seem to know what to do.

The applause was not for *me*. It was for my dad, and *who* he was, *what* he stood for, and how he made people feel about themselves.

He gave us a glimpse into the heart of God. People appreciated the lens.

We sometimes hear people say, "Where *is* the heart of God?" The heart of God is found in the parable of the Good Samaritan, neighbor helping neighbor. And it's not just His compassionate heart that we partake of; it's His hands and feet, too. We get a glimpse into the heart of God when we love one another unconditionally, when we freely forgive others, and when we let Him take our emptiness away and fill our lives with hope. Isn't it beautiful, when we can get that glimpse through our interactions with others? It's a beautiful life lesson.

I didn't talk about my dad's professional accomplishments or his trophies. His obituary covered that stuff. I talked about his faith, his beliefs, and what he taught his family. I gave a funeral homily.

When I stationed myself at the back of the church, after the service, many people who approached me said my homily had inspired them to be better, to be gentler, to engage in life more fully. People told me that the homily had *activated* something within them to return to church or temple and to have a relationship with God. It was really my dad's life that had done that; it was what I had channeled when I was up there, speaking. It was my father who had done this for them, through the things he had taught me and through what he'd given us all.

One of the oddities of my dad's passing was that I *so* wanted to be consoled but found myself in the unusual position of being consoler-in-chief at that moment, and in the days and weeks and months ahead. It was utterly exhausting.

Over 100 cars were in the funeral procession that wound through and around the streets of South Boston, down to Castle

Island, as is tradition, and past our family home before making its way to the cemetery.

It was a beautiful day: fresh air, clear skies, warm sun. It was a perfect golf day. How I longed to be on Cape Cod with Dad. I longed to be anyplace but there.

I had been to a cemetery—many cemeteries—before, but never in a limousine, never behind a hearse, and never for my father, whom I loved so very much. How often do we drive by them, or even take a walk through them, and focus more on the landscaping or stone wall rather than on those who have been welcomed back to the earth? And yet, once you've experienced a cemetery in *this* way, it changes how you look at them. They are quiet, peaceful, and offer us a peek at mortality. They are places of soulful reflection, where headstones stand guard though their once-meaningful epitaphs fade.

I have visited my father almost every day since he died, having skirted frosted leaves, maneuvered around black ice, and run from wild turkeys (no kidding). I weed, fertilize, and trim the grass, adhering—more or less—to the imaginary lot line that surrounds him. I also use the marker for section thirty-six as base camp for a periodic, brisk, three-mile walk. And with this new lens, I notice gravestones in a way I never noticed them before. On every walk, I can't help but Google one name to find out what happened to them. Did the six-year-old die of childhood cancer? Did the eighteen-year-old die in a car crash, or from a drug overdose? How is the family of the policeman who was shot at age thirty-three doing? How is that husband managing, whose wife had a heart attack at fifty-two, leaving behind four high school kids? What was the secret of someone who died at 101? These people have become my friends, and I pray the rosary for them as I walk and check work email. I feel close to my father in this place, though others can't help but remind me he is not there.

We sat in front of my dad's casket on folded chairs atop a green, artificial grass rug, the raw emotion of that memory seared into my mind forever. It's interesting how the funeral director doesn't let the mourners graveside until the casket has been removed from the hearse and the flowers set aside it, hiding the six-foot hole and vault below. I recalled times when, as the deacon, I saw behind the curtain as I waited alongside the gravediggers for the family to arrive, aware that the cemetery workers were a little rough with the casket, telling jokes, making small talk, sipping coffee, assessing the number of cars in the funeral procession, to evaluate how long it would be before the box would be in the ground, so they could keep their day moving.

I cannot remember the words spoken by Fr. Casey, but I remember they were just right. I remember holding my mother's hand, just as my dad had done many times before. I remember my boys' hands on my shoulders, offering strength in a way that was usually reversed. I looked around and wondered—when compared to those others in attendance—whether my family was dressed black *enough*.

Location, location, location. My dad has a good plot, in a good spot, and what was once desolate is now populated with other neighbors—some older, some far too young—and a large shade tree with which my dad's dermatologist would be pleased.

The back of his headstone reads simply, "All Is Well."

PART TWO

Love, Faith, and Education

On October 27, 2004, just days before Halloween, the hallowed Boston Red Sox won the World Series for the first time since 1918, breaking the so-called "Curse of the Bambino" that had followed them for eighty-six years. Sweeping the series in four games, it was an easy win against the St. Louis Cardinals, and Red Sox Nation roared.

The Red Sox had been one of the most successful professional baseball franchises of all time, racking up five World Series titles before 1920.

And then the team made a disastrous decision that would resonate for many years. During the 1919-1920 off-season, the Red Sox sold Babe Ruth, nicknamed The Bambino, for $125,000, to the New York Yankees.

The curse was born. Over and over, year after year, the Red Sox *almost* won but never did. The Yankees went on to become the most successful baseball team of the twentieth century, winning twenty-five championships between 1923 and 1999.

And then, in 2004, the Red Sox's bad luck took a turn for the better.

My dad and I were in Fenway Park for some of those unforgettable World Series moments, as well as the American League Championship Series playoff games against, of course, their archrivals, the New York Yankees. He loved baseball talk under the lights, and often told stories of Ted Williams, Carlton Fisk, Carl Yastrzemski, Rico Petrocelli, Johnny Pesky, Dwight Evans . . . and Babe Ruth.

I grew up with my dad telling the tale that we were related to the Babe. He never explained it; it was always said in a fun, comical manner. At times, at family parties, one of my cousins would come up to me and say, "Did you know we were related to Babe Ruth?" So my father wasn't the only one telling the story. Many family members in his generation were in agreement about it.

After my father's passing, we solved the mystery once and for all. My father's Aunt Sis, the remarkable lady who raised him, had a slew of brothers and sisters. They were beautiful people, by every account. Her brother, Kevin P. Tighe, married Mary A. Woodford. Mary was the sister of Mary Ellen (Helen) Woodford, who was Babe Ruth's first wife. When Ruth was a rookie with the Red Sox, Helen was a sixteen-year-old waitress from South Boston working in Lander's Coffee Shop, which the Babe would sometimes frequent for bacon and eggs. The young couple married in 1914 and moved to a large farm in Sudbury—but the marriage, by many accounts, was a troubled one from the start. They separated in the 1920s, and Helen died tragically in a house fire in Watertown, Massachusetts, in 1929.

So, the Babe wasn't a cousin, but he was in the family. And we, of course, were happy to have him for *no* less a reason than good storytelling rights.

It seemed that my dad never really had a childhood of his own, and in many ways he lived his early years vicariously through me, my kids, and maybe even a bit through Babe Ruth and the rest of the league. And, in both an ironic twist and bookend, my dad lived out the end of his days with Lou Gehrig's disease, named after the Iron Horse of the New York Yankees for seventeen seasons, in what turned out—for my family and others'—to be another curse.

My father always taught me that all you can give your children are love, faith, and education, and that everything else in life was a bonus. He reminded me of this responsibility often in both word and deed.

How do we love our kids?

It's a big question, and not every parent will agree on the answer. Some might say, "Be their friend." Others might say, "We're not their friends; we're their parents." The debate is endless, but the debate is not the objective. Maybe we can at least agree that it starts with acceptance of who they are. We love our children when we stop trying to fix them, when we stop trying to make them into everything that we wanted to be or chose not to be. We are called to inspire them and let them fly.

And when they fall? How many times do we lift them up? Seven times seventy and seventy times more.

"Preach the Gospel at all times. When necessary, use words."
What a beautiful reminder from St. Francis of Assisi.

One of my all-time favorite movie scenes is from *Evan Almighty*, a 2007 comedy about a family in crisis, all of them busy ark-building and getting the animals lined up two-by-two. When newscaster Evan Baxter, played by Steve Carell, faces personal and professional challenges of biblical proportions, his wife, played by Lauren Graham, leaves him and takes the kids. She can't grasp his new calling as a modern-day Noah. In a restaurant, she encounters God, played by Morgan Freeman, and he both challenges and inspires her to return to her husband.

"If someone prays for patience," says God, disguised as a busboy, "do you think God gives them patience? Or does He give them the opportunity to be patient?" After elaborating on this briefly, he says, "If someone prayed for the family to be closer, do you think God zaps them with warm fuzzy feelings, or does He give them opportunities to love each other?" Maybe, for something so complex, loving our children is that simple.

Some of the hardest days with our kids are those when they could use a little more care, concern, hope, empathy, compassion, and emotional intelligence from *us*. Perhaps God gives us the opportunities to demonstrate those gifts and to exercise those muscles. Perhaps we embrace those most difficult days as ways to love our children *more*. What we know is that kids blossom when they feel unconditionally loved.

What is the gift of faith?

I grew up in a faith-filled family—whatever that means. We were *hardly* religious fanatics. We went to church, abstained from meat on Fridays during Lent, and the Infant of Prague took a dominant position in the parlor. I remember Jesus being covered with a clear vinyl tent that, I guess—in hindsight—was supposed to keep the dust off but looked more like some sort of COVID hazmat suit. My dad read the Bible—along with John Grisham and James Patterson—and all the bedroom lamps were affixed with rosary beads. I was blessed to be able to attend both Catholic grammar and high schools.

But how do we *really* give faith?

God has given us the gift of desire. He planted it in all of us. We desire many things. Maybe we desire more family time, love, a job, a *better* job, good health, fewer emails, a vacation, retirement, fewer aches and pains. Maybe we desire a baby, a cure for ALS or cancer, more time, or a good night's sleep. Or maybe we desire just a little peace and quiet. How does that sound?

Helping our kids figure out what they desire is one of a parent's most important calls to action. What if we taught our children that what they *mostly* desire is God? To come to know Him, to seek Him, to be in a relationship with Him, and to love Him. What if we taught our kids that our desire for God is written on their hearts? And with Him, we see *everything* differently.

I wonder how planting that seed would affect their optics on life. I wonder if that would give them better prospects at an awesome marriage. I wonder if it would give them more of a chance at recognizing our affordable housing, substance abuse, inequality, or climate change crises, and maybe want to help. I wonder if they might be quicker to stop their car on a cold, snowy afternoon when a shivering homeless person is standing at a red light holding a sign. Never mind a few bucks; would our children offer their coat or hat?

We all have an individual path to God. We all have our own brand of holiness and reverence and way to act it out. People could see my father's brand on his face. It was an afterglow, and "Afterglow" is the name of the poem we put on his Mass card.

By finding God, our personalities are made fuller and richer. St. Thomas Aquinas spent his entire life surrounded by books, while St. Francis told his friars not to own even one, so as not to become proud. There are many, many roads to God, and few of them are straight.

Desire is what my parents taught me about faith. It seemed that no matter how fulfilled I felt, something was missing. At times I thought I was just hungry, with an emptiness in my belly; at other times it felt like a certain longing. And then I responded to Christ. I found hope in His promise in all that I do.

Bruce Springsteen had it right: we all have hungry hearts.

How do you give someone an education?

On the surface, it means getting them into the right school—whatever that means—or paying for someone's tuition. Maybe it's funding a 529 plan, a tax-advantaged investment program used to pay higher education costs. No question, we all want the best education for our kids, and providing them with a good education gives them a gateway to something better, maybe something more than we had. In today's fast-changing world, formal education is especially important.

When my father taught me the lesson that all you can give your kids is love, faith, and education, I thought *formal* education was *only* what he meant. Along the way, I came to learn that was only a *very* small part of it. Our children are always learning.

How we speak to our spouses teaches our kids about marriage. Trying to "beat the system" teaches our kids about honesty. Getting someone to punch out early for us teaches our kids about work ethic. Every day, we teach our kids about pride, envy, gossip, and anger. And every day we have an opportunity to teach our kids about hospitality, goodness, compassion, and courage. They're watching us *very* carefully, whether we think so or not.

We educate our kids by our own examples, whatever examples we choose to give them, intentionally or not. My dad taught my kids how to play cribbage, chess, and golf, but that was all merely an entertaining head-fake. He was really teaching them about the importance of savoring time with family. My father may have taken my kids along for the ride to do an errand and drop something off at the shelter, but what he was really teaching them was how to feed the hungry. My father didn't speak often at office meetings, but by not speaking he was teaching me that being a good listener made its own potent impact.

And lots of teaching happened at Fenway Park. My dad had been a Boston Red Sox season ticketholder for over a quarter-century, Section 31 Box 162. Many memories still sit in those seats along third base. I still have, sitting in a drawer, the unperforated tickets from the 2020 pandemic season that never was. There were many warm days and many more cold nights, seasons that ended way too early from our own shortcomings, and seasons that should have ended differently. But they were all memorable, in my family's eyes. I think about all the father-son-grandson-granddaughter talks that happened over a hot dog or a slice of pizza.

———————

No matter who went to what game, my dad always reserved Patriot's Day for himself and my mom. It was a tradition. Any one of us may have been fortunate to attend opening day, but Patriots' Day was, well, *sacred sacrum*. The ritual was the same: They caught the Sox at Fenway Park, located at about mile twenty-five of the Boston Marathon. They left the game at about the fifth or sixth inning, depending how the Sox were doing, and then they walked down Boylston Street to catch part of the race excitement.

The game also coordinated with the end of tax season. Well into his seventies, my dad worked long days during the winters, and *this* game meant the start of easier summer days to come.

But one year was different. On April 15, 2013, two homemade pressure cooker bombs exploded a couple hundred yards apart near the finish line, killing three people and injuring several hundred others. It was the deadliest terrorist attack on domestic soil since 9/11.

My folks were a couple of blocks from where the explosions occurred. What if the crowds were smaller that day and moved faster, or what if my parents' hand-in-hand stroll had been more of a brisk walk? They would have been right on top of it, five to seven minutes later.

Did God intervene? Maybe that day—for His *own* reasons—He did.

For the next five days, not only was Boston on edge, but parts of it were also on lockdown. The Boston Red Sox became a symbol of the city's resilience. We became Boston Strong, and the Sox went on to win the World Series, letting the nation know that Boston was all about its inner strength, recovering quickly and moving forward.

The Boston Marathon bombing changed us. Every year, as the marathon concludes, it's less about the winner but a reminder of a city's triumph. In many ways, over a half-century apart, sports helped to heal an entire city and continued to heal a kid from Southie.

Lou Gehrig signed on with the New York Yankees in 1923 and played 2,130 consecutive games, a record that stood for fifty-six years until it was surpassed by Cal Ripken Jr. in 1995.

Gehrig's streak continued until 1939 when he took himself out of the lineup, shocking his fans, teammates, and the league. He was growing weaker but didn't know why. His performance had been significantly compromised, and he was later diagnosed with ALS, forcing him into retirement at the age of thirty-six. At his iconic farewell address at Yankee Stadium, Gehrig said, "I consider myself the luckiest man on the face of the Earth."

He died on June 2, 1941, just about six months after my father was born. Upon hearing the news, my "cousin," Babe Ruth, and his second wife, Claire, were one of the first visitors to the Gehrig family home. And on June 2, 2021, exactly eighty years later, Major League Baseball launched its first annual Lou Gehrig Day to honor him and raise awareness for ALS.

Family Makes the Difference

Family makes the difference in the good life well-lived. Family grounds us, challenges us, enjoys us, encourages us, and nurtures us. It gives us people to listen to and confide in.

Sure, our families can drive us nuts, too. But believe it or not, having a family in our lives causes us to live longer, be happier, and enables us to live our *best life evah*. There are lessons to be learned in the richness and sustenance of family.

I appreciate that everyone has a different experience with their family. I have been blessed with good memories, even if I choose to romanticize some of them. And yet we don't need to turn on the television to know that in families there is alcoholism and drug abuse, desertion, neglect, mental illness, and much more. These were not part of my experience, though I know in my travels as a deacon that nobody knows what really goes on behind our friends' manicured lawns, beautiful front doors, and Irish lace curtains.

Love is never free; we all know that. Even the most perfect house has some cracked walls. And there have been many times I have stood at the back of church when a parishioner has approached me and said, "Deacon Kevin, do you have a second?" Those conversations were sometimes hard, tears were sometimes shared, and those houses were sometimes prisons filled with fear, seesawing back and forth between tension and calm, between abuse and reconciliation.

When my father died, many family members, and close friends who are like family, stepped in and lifted us up. I have no brothers and sisters, and I had never been more sad, anxious, and disheartened in my entire life.

But in came a steady stream of calls and text messages, books on grief, sympathy cards, and brief notes that would show up in my mailbox. We got wonderful invitations to dinner, offers to meet halfway for pizza on a Saturday night, invitations to watch football games on Sunday afternoons. These were heartfelt reaches into the depths of my despair, and they shall never be forgotten.

Grief is hard. It comes in waves. Some are little waves, and some are so big they sweep you away. It's shocking and numbing. Grief is personal and changes you forever. It forces you to stretch your heart *and* your mind. Grief comes out of a bond that survives death and has a convenient way of removing us from the present moment. No two people grieve the same way, or in the same order. Once the loss starts to sink in, there's a bombardment of emotions, from fear to uncertainty to agitation to bewilderment, and tons more. And once the funeral is over, that's when the grievers need family and friends the most.

Grief is a great team sport. My best advice? Don't disappear after the funeral; reach out. *Keep* reaching out. It means a lot—*more* than you know. And when we don't call or text back? Don't take it personally. It means we're in a funk, but *keep trying*. Please, *keep trying*.

I know. We're all busy. We don't know what to say. We don't know what to do. We don't want to be a bother. We thought you bounced back after a long weekend. I guess if you've never experienced grief, it's hard to relate. But this much we do know: once we have come to know more about death than we wish we had to, we come to know about life in ways that we never thought possible.

———————

For months after my father died, I walked around in a fog. I was beyond sad. I mostly didn't miss a day, visiting the cemetery where he lay. ACL surgery and snow don't mix well, and they did keep me away for a couple of weeks. I had this crazy idea that if I didn't visit my father he would think I had abandoned him. I was afraid that I would forget him, that his memory would start to become a blur, and that he would quickly become something of my past. Some people say that the past is the past, and that was my fear. Visiting my dad was my way of keeping the past in the present, keeping him alive, and keeping him close both physically and emotionally.

I know, I know, it doesn't make sense. Or maybe it does.

I decided to put one foot in front of the other, and this time not in the direction of my father's grave. I'd tried to do this, unsuccessfully, many times before, but hadn't willed myself to attend the bereavement group at the local chapter of The ALS Association.

It was the week before Christmas. The holiday lights and songs and parties were weighing me down, and a little support was *exactly* what I needed. I'd never been to a support group, so I didn't know what to expect. From watching the movie *Anger Management*, I envisioned a large circle with metal folding chairs and a strategically placed folding table with a coffee urn—OK, I never quite thought about it like that before—and Entenmann's chocolate chip cookies lined up in a couple of tidy rows on a plastic tray. If there was an overflow, maybe there would be a second row of chairs, and that's where I would sit.

I had it all planned out in my head. I was *not* going to speak. I was just going to listen and nod with genuine empathy. I was excited—not really—but I was going on a field trip and these likeminded people would know *exactly* what I was going through and make it better. They would help fix my pain.

The meeting started at 6:30, but traffic caused me to be late, arriving at 6:40. But when I showed, there were only two cars in the parking lot. *What?* I figured one was an ALS family member and the other was The ALS Association staff member, facilitating the evening.

Was everyone running late? Traffic *was* a little snarly. *What should I do?* I waited. *What should I do?* Ten more minutes passed. I opened my door, and at that exact moment two people came out of the building, got into their cars, and drove off. *What? What just happened?*

I called Lisa, in tears, and she pressed me to know why I was crying. I said, "I'm not sure what just happened, but I think I'm mourning the loss of my bereavement group, and I've never even met them."

Both of my parents are from large families—though my mom's family is smaller today than it once was, as life's end has taken its share. It has a way of doing that. Oddly enough, though, I am an only child.

Only children sometimes get a bad rap. They're considered self-absorbed, bossy, antisocial, and lonely. I would like to think I'm none of those things. I'm not asking you to take a poll—I already did that and, like Sally Field, I learned that "You like me, you *really* like me." People jumped all over Sally Field for her 1985 Oscar acceptance speech, but after the brouhaha quieted down everyone realized what her comment meant, which is simply that we all want to belong to something bigger than ourselves. We all want to belong to a family, no matter how we define it. My dad did, Sally did, I do. We all do.

And, sure, there's no question that my parents, especially my mom, thought that the sun rose and set over me. And, you know, there's nothing wrong with that thought. It's a tough world out there, and kids need their parents to be their biggest fans. They need cheerleaders, and they need people in their lives who encourage them and love them in absolute ways. My parents did exactly that. If it seems *too* perfect, it was.

I married the love of my life, Lisa Carbone, on October 13, 1991. Muse, friend, lover, teacher, protector, listener, mystic, advisor, and the yin to my yang. We met in 1985 at Bentley College, now Bentley University—the other "BU." She's the oldest of five, and I could not have married into a more loving family. In a 2017 interview, Berkshire Hathaway CEO Warren Buffet said that the most important decision you'll ever make has nothing to do with money or career. He said the biggest decision of your life will be whom you choose to marry. I chose *very* well.

We honeymooned for close to three years on the water at Marina Bay in Quincy, Massachusetts—known as the "City of Presidents." John Adams, and his son John Quincy Adams, as well as John Hancock, the first signer of the Declaration of Independence, called Quincy home.

As the area developed, our rent quickly rose, and we moved into my mom and dad's two-family house in Southie. Their home was in the perfect South Boston location. It was detached from the houses on both sides of it, with a front yard, backyard, two-car garage, and a good-size *pahlah*, which is Boston pronunciation for parlor or living room. It was a block from the beach and had a view of the JFK Presidential Library from the second-floor porch. It was the perfect walking distance to Castle Island and back. And it was filled with love.

Castle Island is a peninsula in Southie on the shore of Boston Harbor. Sitting on twenty-two acres, it's the oldest fortified military site in British North America. It's also home to walking trails, a fishing pier, a playground, a beach, and Sully's, a local takeout landmark.

Castle Island is one of those special places where you can always be assured of a cool breeze, a friendly face, and beautiful views of ships traveling through the harbor and planes landing at Logan Airport.

Lisa was pregnant with our son, Kevin. We only intended to stay in Southie for a year or so until we found something of our own. Then Connor came along. Then Brian. And rumor had it that Lisa was pregnant again. My wonderful father-in-law, Peter,

Sicilian through and through, said to me, "If it's a girl, I hope she's going to be named Gina Lollobrigida!" Then Meghan came along.

The kids grew up especially close to my parents during those early years. The living quarters cemented a foundation of love and support that multiplied a hundredfold. It was the classic three-generation home, with food and people always in motion up and down the front and back stairs. Kids would go down. Meatloaf would come up. Kids would come up. Chicken pot pie would go down. Kids would go down. Shepherd's pie would come up. And, at times, nobody knew where the kids were, but hamburgers and hot dogs would come in from the grill and the kids would magically appear. By the time we moved out, a decade later, we had four kids in one eight-by-eight bedroom—upper bunk, lower bunk, trundle, and toddler bed. It was the best of times. It was *only* the best of times.

My father was always close to his brothers, cousins, aunts, and uncles. When I was growing up, I recall many Sunday afternoon trips with my mom and dad after church for tea and donuts or sandwiches, at the homes of the many loving aunts and uncles who had informally raised and nurtured him growing up. When I look back, I see they were bigger than life. Those were precious days, and I didn't realize how precious they were until many years later.

There's a great, fast-paced, foot-stomping Irish tune called "McNamara's Band." It's over a hundred years old. And if you've ever been to an Irish party—a hooley—you've certainly heard it. In the chorus, McNamara, the leader of the band, tells us about all the band members and the bounty of instruments they play.

Oh, the drums go bang and the cymbals clang and the horns they blaze away.
McCarthy pumps the old bassoon and I the pipes do play.
And Hennessy Tennessy tootles the flute and the music is something grand,
a credit to old Ireland is McNamara's Band.

And in many ways, that was my dad's family. There were lots of gatherings and family parties growing up. The rug would get rolled up, someone would sit at the piano, guitars would get hauled out of the trunks of cars, tambourines would get pulled from closet shelves, and my dad's kazoo would emerge from its forever-home in his shirt pocket. And so, there were Martins and Connollys and Staffords, too, and Sheehys, McCabes, and Wirtanens all through—and, of course, the McKennas from across the pond—a credit to another family generation that made sure that everyone stayed *very* close.

The Firm

I had the pleasure of working with my dad at the firm for over thirty-five years. We were business partners, among some other fine and upstanding people, in one of the largest New England CPA and consulting practices.

Working with my father was the highlight of my professional career. Nothing else comes close, nothing at all. I would give anything—anything at all—to have those days back.

My dad was always in the office early, especially during the so-called "tax season." During that time of year, even his last season, he still put in sixty-hour workweeks, at least six days a week. My dad was more introverted than I, but spent a lot of time walking through the office, engaging with team members. I am more outgoing, but I do not often venture far from my office. I know that when I do I am besieged with "have-a-minute" questions for hours. It throws my day off. Maybe that is supposed to *be* my day?

As I look back, I know that the KPM team enjoyed that "stop and talk" quality about my dad, and it was one way that I wish I had been more like him. And unbeknownst to me at the time, my favorite part of the day was when my dad's walk around the office would find him in *my* office, and he would sit down in a chair or on the couch and we would catch up on just about anything. Unless I was on the phone, for him, I always got up and came around my desk and sat for a few minutes. We may have talked about cash collections, client invoices that needed to go out, human resource matters, client projects, scheduling . . . or it may have been about weekend plans. He made it all look so easy . . . as easy as riding a bike. Whatever we talked about, it was perfect.

My dad started the business with another partner in 1968, next to a bowling alley in Weymouth Landing, Massachusetts. In those days, it was mostly a bookkeeping and 1040 shop with four or five employees.

From when I was seven or eight years old, I remember the glass storefront, the half-dead potted plants in the windows, the musty smell of the file room, and the clickety-clack and ringing bells of a long line of IBM Selectric typewriters. I remember the brown paneling and the sound and vibration of the bowling pin reset machine next door. Occasionally, you could hear the cheers and jeers of friends mocking a pal's coordination or candlepin abilities.

And yet it was a practical setup. "It was efficient," my dad would remind me with a wink and a smile.

I joined the practice in 1989, about twenty years after its founding, and after my own brief but gratifying stint at Peat Marwick, now KPMG, one of the world's largest accounting firms. My mom and dad were very proud of my recruitment to KPMG, presenting me with my first briefcase for my birthday just a month before my start date. I can still smell the brown leather, and I remember the cushy handle, and the raised, gold-embossed initials, "KPM." It didn't take long for it to get weathered, beaten and scarred—from all the hard work, I convinced myself.

The transition to my father's practice wasn't easy. It was tough—very tough. It was difficult coming into an established business in an entry-level position as a family member of one of the owners.

It was *so* hard that my dad eventually separated from his original partner. His partner was a good man, also from South Boston. Our families had been friends, and my dad was troubled by that separation for a long time.

Second-generation companies often *don't* make it. Maybe the reins never quite get turned over, maybe the second generation never quite gets welcomed or trained or doesn't have the same drive or ambition as the first generation.

Unfortunately, we see this all the time in our own client base. Family members, especially kids, get forced into the business. There's tremendous pressure to carry on the legacy, whatever that might be. A few kids have the knack for it; many others don't. Some work at it, many others don't. Some want to follow other paths, but still want the fancy perks, like premium health insurance and auto allowances. Existing family feuds can get exacerbated. Nepotism can be a source of resentment among non-family members, causing frustration and high turnover. And all those perceived inequities and built-up emotions can result in countless problems along the way.

At the office, my father—always practical—would sometimes be critical of what he perceived as "overthinking it." Usually with a full plate, he would occasionally leave a team meeting that appeared to be going nowhere and later commenting to me, "You guys go round 'n' round and don't make any decisions."

"Houston, we have an overengineering problem." Consulting firms sometimes over-engineer projects because what they are trying to build is the *wrong* thing. Rather than focus on what the customer *needs*, they focus on what they think the customer *wants*. That notion often gets applied to internal projects as well.

Through the years, I've seen many enterprise resource projects (ERP) get off-track when people try to implement every bell and whistle of a piece of software because the platform or system has the capability. In the short term, with limited capital, the client just wants to evaluate a few integral outcomes, for example: What does my domestic staffing plan look like if we increase international sales by 15 percent? What are the necessary, point-of-sale (POS) features needed to reduce theft and inventory shrinkage by 2 percent? What are the key performance indicators (KPIs) that can help to measure innovation outputs?

The pandemic changed everything; you know that. We had five offices and a coast-to-coast platform in the not-for-profit, affordable housing, and film and entertainment industries. The world had been swept up in a whirlwind of social, economic, political, and spiritual transformation. That transformation included the accounting industry. The business symptoms of

COVID-19 included staff burnout, remote hiring challenges, downsizing of office space, and more flexible working schedules. The pressure was on to reinvent, be more innovative, expand market share, create sustainable and inclusive growth, make a substantial investment in technology, and leverage overseas talent to offset rising business costs. And although COVID metastasized into multiple variations and strains, the economy flourished, access to capital swelled, and private equity pushed into the accounting industry, resulting in the combination of many top, name-brand firms.

After considerable discussion and debate, two years after my dad died, assessing both the opportunities and threats, the KPM shareholders voted to combine the practice with a national accounting and consulting firm headquartered in New York. Although it was a very emotional decision, the data supported it, and my dad would have been pleased, knowing that though we went round 'n' round, we made a good decision with a sharp eye to the future. It was a decision that better enabled us to respond to marketplace demands, expansion opportunities, more geographic resources, and industry expertise.

I am a senior partner in the new company, and it feels like family to me. The combination allows me to make a larger and more substantial impact on the profession. My dad knew one of the now-deceased namesakes of my new firm from their shared work in affordable housing. He and my dad were kind and accomplished men, and they had a history of trust and mutual respect. Taking a lesson from Dad's playbook, the combination was a practical and simple decision that seized the moment in the time that was before us. Sometimes *less* is more. Sometimes *simple* is more. Sometimes the obvious decision *is* the most strategic. My father always reminded the company team of the higher value of the more practical proposition. "It's the better answer 90 percent of the time," he would say.

Life with Mom

My mom would put her right arm carefully around my neck, tell me how much she loved me, and we would skip through our South Boston, three-room apartment as she sang, "A Bushel and a Peck." It was always about me.

The song, written by Frank Loesser, was introduced in the Broadway musical *Guys and Dolls*. And though there have been over a dozen recorded versions, it was Doris Day that my mom impersonated. She would tell you herself, however, that carrying a tune was not her strong suit.

"Hey, do you know where I can get a henway?" my father would sometimes ask.

"What's a henway?" any one of us would answer, knowing the punchline already.

"Oh, about two to three pounds," he would respond, hysterical, as if he had never told the joke before.

Similarly, what's a bushel and a peck? It means "a lot." My mom loves me a lot, and I love her "more." It's something like a running joke between us, that we talk like this, that I insist I love her "more." I have a similar one with my daughter, Meghan. When I tell my mom by text, almost every night, that I love her more than a bushel and a peck, she likes to write back, "No waaaay."

My mother, Claire Marie (Sullivan) Martin was born on August 17, 1940 to Henry and Anna Sullivan, both of Irish descent. Not only does she share her birthday with Maureen O'Hara, she also shares it with Robert DeNiro, Sean Penn, beloved cousin Paul Sheehy, and *my* first pastor after I was ordained, Fr. Arthur Wright.

She's the youngest of four, three girls and a boy—the opposite of Lisa and me. Her older sister, Carol, and her family live not too far away, close enough that my mom can see Carol whenever she wants. Her older brother, Bobby, was a WWII veteran, stationed on the USS *Valley Forge*. He lived in Massillon, Ohio, just fifteen minutes from the Pro Football Hall of Fame. He and his wife, Mary, are buried in the same cemetery as my dad, and a trip to see my dad *usually* means a trip to see my Uncle Bob. My mother's aunt Kathleen, my grandmother's sister, never married. She is buried in the same plot as my father. She didn't want to be alone for eternity, so my folks bought their burial plot when "Kat" died. Many of my parents' family members are in the same cemetery, all within a few hundred yards of each other. My mother's oldest sister, Eleanor, died many years ago from Alzheimer's. One of Eleanor's children, Ann, also my godmother, works at the firm, too, and sits just outside my office.

My mom is five-foot-two, with eyes of brown, weighing in at 102 pounds soaking wet. Sometimes she wears a petite size two.

Did you realize there is a petite size zero? There is, and that is what she wears those *other* times. She has the quintessential Boston accent, right out of central casting. There are no R's in her vocabulary. Car is "cah." Far is "fah." Supper is "suppah." How are you is "howahyah." If it's anything, it's authentic.

Don't underestimate her size; she is the protector and defender. Mess with my family and it is my mother with whom you will contend, and it won't be pretty. I can promise you that. She protected my dad . . . and she protects me, my wife, and kids. When I was young, I once had a new bike that my dad had been teaching me how to ride over the course of a few days. You're right, he didn't know how to ride a bike—but he was a good teacher. One afternoon, a couple of kids came up to me at the front sidewalk, admired the bike . . . *and stole it*. It all happened very fast. I yelled, "Ma," and Ma came quickly to the front porch. And once she realized what was happening, she took off on foot and chased those kids through two yards, and over one very tall fence.

Let's just say, I got the bike back, and *it* didn't have a scratch on it.

Family means everything to my mother, and because of that I grew up with the greatest childhood imaginable. When I was young, she stayed at home to care for me. She didn't "work," as some people call it. And I guess that's true. She didn't work for money, she worked for love. She played teacher, nurse, chef, cleaner, mechanic, and sports coach.

Another song I remember my mom singing to me is "Too Ra Loo Ra Loo Ral," also known as "That's an Irish Lullaby." The song was made famous by Bing Crosby in 1944's *Going My Way*. I also remember my mom singing this song to my kids when they were babies, and for many years after.

Over in Killarney
Many years ago,
Me Mither sang a song to me
In tones so sweet and low.
Just a simple little ditty,
In her good ould Irish way,
And I'd give the world if she could sing
That song to me this day.
"Too-ra-loo-ra-loo-ral, Too-ra-loo-ra-li,
Too-ra-loo-ra-loo-ral, hush now, don't you cry!
Too-ra-loo-ra-loo-ral, Too-ra-loo-ra-li,
Too-ra-loo-ra-loo-ral, that's an Irish lullaby.

When my kids were young, my mother and father babysat on a regular basis. My mom babysat certain days of the week so Lisa could work, as did Lisa's very kind and affable mother, Carol. And my mom and dad sometimes babysat so Lisa and I could get out to dinner or a movie or away for a long weekend. We were tired—four kids under eight will do that sometimes. My mom lived for those times with my kids, and made a big deal of it.

Lisa and I went to the movies, once, and bumped into my parents with the kids going to a different movie. "Oh, we figured we would go for a ride and get pizza and somehow ended up here," she said. "You weren't supposed to see us."

It was through those early days living in the same house that my mom became so close to my kids, and that bond continues to this day. She calls them "Love," and since my father died, *they* check in on *her*.

And love is the lesson, her lesson. Before my dad passed away, pre-COVID, it was not unusual for my mother to text me and say, "I'm taking Meg out shopping and for lunch. Talk later." My mom lives twenty minutes from my house, so visits are easy, as are snow-shoveling, hedge-trimming, and minor chores. We all remain incredibly close, "minus one."

I know where I stand with my mother. If you know her, you do, too. She pulls no punches and holds little back. We are similar. My mother and I are very much the same in so many ways, and restraint is not our most impressive quality.

She's honest, wise, selfless, religious, concerned, and generous. She hardly ever comes to our house empty-handed. "I left a bag on the counter," she will say. "There's two articles I cut out for you. One of them is on statins. You've been on Lipitor too long. You really should figure out a way to get off them. And there's two bags of Lay's potato chips. I made stuffed mushrooms, there's sixteen of them. You just have to heat them up."

When my father split from his original business partner, my mom joined the practice. She has a windowed, private office outside my dad's now barren office. Human resources, payroll, accounts payable—through the years, she's done all of it. She is impeccably dressed, always. The office feels very different without my dad. My mother, who still works for KPM as I wind down administrative operations, sometimes calls me in the morning before work and says, "I'm making a tuna fish sandwich for lunch, do you want one?" She enjoys taking care of people. That's what she does—and she cleans. She cleans a lot. I wish I owned stock in Swiffer.

"Yes, tuna sounds good," I would always say. "You know how I like it."

"Yeah, I know . . . onion and too much mayonnaise. You should check your blood pressure, it's probably high. And all I have is gluten-free bread, is that okay?"

"That's fine." The gluten-free bread *isn't* terrible—and I *was* getting a free tuna sandwich.

"I will bring you some chips," she would say.

"I don't want chips. You just gave us some chips."

"Okay, I will bring you some chips."

She is still very much on her game. She may not have a college degree, but she's got street smarts—Southie street smarts—and those street smarts have served her—and all of us—well. She has a sense of people. It might be good, or it might be bad, but no matter, she's usually right. And protecting the family means paying attention. If an office shredding invoice says, "Shred six bins," she will call the company and say, "How could you shred six bins? We only have five bins." She tells me, "I'm protecting you just like I protected your father." I sometimes ride my bike to work, and let's agree: nobody better try stealing it.

My mother cooked; she still does. It wasn't fancy food. It was comfort food, and it was delicious. Even now, cooking for one, she makes herself a big *suppah* every night. We didn't eat fast food. Sure, McDonald's was a periodic treat, coming home from the pediatrician's office. But I grew up on roast beef or turkey dinners on Sundays. Meatloaf, chicken, pork roast, pork chops. Fish not so much.

Sometimes we would have breakfast for dinner. Potatoes—pronounced *b'daydas*—there were always potatoes. There are *still* always potatoes.

My mom and I think with our hearts. Unlike my dad, the data doesn't *always* matter to us. That can be a good—and a bad thing. The good thing is that we both care a lot; our love is thick. The bad thing, at times, is that our mouths sometimes move faster than our brains. Does that ever get us in trouble? Sure. But that trouble fixes itself quickly.

My mom loves the holidays—or she did before my dad died. She honors tradition. She makes corned beef and cabbage on St. Patrick's Day—grey corned beef, never red. She grins from ear to ear while my kids open their Christmas or birthday presents, because she went to great lengths to get "just the right thing."

I still remember calling her on Sundays during the holiday season, and asking what she was doing. She might respond, "I'm wrapping, your father is reading the paper, and we are watching a movie. I've got beef stew on the stove." There was a sound of contentment in her voice, that sound no longer there.

And the family trips? They are her favorites.

Some kids talk to their parents a few times a month. I talk to my mom at least a few times a day—literally; morning, noon, and night.

Here's a thought: Let's say your mom or dad has another five years to live. And let's say you only see or talk to them two to three times a year.

Think about that in a different way. Your parents may live another five years, but you're only going to talk with them another ten to fifteen times.

Maybe you should pick up that phone. A phone call can be as powerful as a hug, when it has to be.

My mom has changed since my dad died. I understand, though I also don't.

She doesn't smile too much these days. She refuses to put up a Christmas tree. It makes me sad to see her sad. And the pandemic didn't help matters.

My mom likes to talk about politics. She enjoys debating with my kids. She continues to give to what she refers to as "your father's charities." My mother is a very strong woman. She, too, is a remarkable lady, and has slowly started to put one foot in front of the other. If I can get a few more smiles and get her to agree to put up a Christmas tree this year, or next, we will have made a lot of progress together.

I love her a bushel and a peck.

The Servant Leader

My father's faith strongly informed and influenced the work he did, and not only in the ways he contributed to the Church and the community. When I look at what he did for the firm where he was president until a month before his death, I see how he embodied the servant leader there and elsewhere.

My dad was frequently the smartest person in the room, though you would *never* know it. He offered insight and perspective and strategy ideas in a calming and quiet manner. I went to him often as my own technical resource. He was able to break down a larger issue into smaller, simpler pieces. He was also the helper. If we had a partner's lunch, he was the one who would go around the conference room with a green trash bag and have people toss in their dirty paper plates and sandwich wrappers, chip bags, and half-eaten pickles. He would do the same after family parties. And on Christmas morning, after all the presents had been torn open, and the wrapping paper was all over the parlor, he was the one on his hands and knees with another green trash bag packing it all up, *every* last piece of it.

The word "deacon" is derived from the Greek word *dia-konos,* meaning "servant." I had always been taught that a good deacon is like the head waiter at a restaurant, like the waiters at the Feast of Cana. It's not your party, and if you do your job well, nobody sees you doing it. In the same way, my dad, albeit informally, played the role of deacon at our company.

Kevin Martin occupied the corner office, but he spent a good part of his day stopping by the offices of others and engaging in conversation in the large, bulky bullpen of cubicles. The drop-ins were short, casual, and purposeful. Sometimes he may have wanted the answer to a question, sometimes he may have wished to offer an idea or perspective or interpretation, but it was mostly just to ask about your weekend or family, or to comment on the Red Sox win or loss from the previous evening. My dad would be the first one to play with a new baby in the company family when a team member out on maternity or paternity leave stopped by to visit with their child.

Deacons are character studies and inspire others to follow. My father, most humbly, was a servant leader. "Whoever wishes to be great among you shall be your servant." (Matthew 20:26)

While Christ may have been the originator of servant leadership, the phrase was coined by Robert K. Greenleaf in "The Servant Leader," an essay he published in 1970. I've seen many definitions of what makes a servant leader, but to put it simply, servant leaders are the shepherds in their organizations. They lead their flocks and everyone around them to green pastures and still waters. Servant leaders have power and influence, but they use it wisely to make their communities better places. And by doing that, they make the world a better place.

They listen. They persuade. They create trust. And along the way, their followers become more learned, grow in wisdom, and become servants themselves.

Since he was young, my father knew that he wanted to serve the larger community, and that is the first criteria in *any* servant leadership model. He wasn't in it for the glamour. He preferred a sweater and corduroys to a fancy suit. And though he had a large office, it was hardly a museum or showplace, unlike my own.

My office is adorned with photos of the people I have met on my own journey. Each photo has a story, and I enjoy retelling every anecdote. My dad's office walls were littered with nails for pictures that had been sitting on his floor for years, since that last time his office was repainted, and he had never gotten around to hanging them back up. Regrettably, neither had I. But my father *was* looking for a quiet platform for good works. And through that platform, the servant leader engages many stakeholders for the betterment of society.

How do we know that we are called to serve? And then, once we think we know, how do we come to realize *how* we are called to serve? What *is* the platform?

It all comes from discernment. Maybe it's a recurring dream, an internal tugging or pulling or debate, or maybe it's that visceral instinct in our gut that we keep trying to ignore. According to Ebenezer Scrooge, it could be some undigested food speaking to us. But no matter what the circumstances, in all our decisions, in all our reflection and contemplation and wondering—even if we don't know it—we are trying to find God's will for us. That's discernment in a nutshell.

I had a long road to the diaconate. Though I only realized it in hindsight, I had been discerning Holy Orders, in some way, since I was at Boston College High School, some forty years earlier. Was God calling me to be a priest? Was He calling me to get married and have a bunch of kids? Was He calling me to be a deacon? Even now that I am ordained, I wonder, what type of deacon is God calling me to be? Where does He want me to spend my time? What social justice issues is He calling me to? How do I do that? I try to bring the answers to these types of questions to my volunteer activities and everyday work.

One of my spiritual influencers was the famous Trappist monk Thomas Merton. He was a writer, theologian, mystic, poet, and social activist. He lived at the Abbey of Gethsemani in Kentucky. I had the opportunity to attend a silent retreat at the abbey in 2013 with my fellow diaconate candidates. Among his more than fifty books, Merton's most famous writing, a national bestseller, was a spiritual autobiography entitled *Seven Story Mountain*, published in 1948. This was a guy who struggled with his faith and was always questioning what God was asking of him. He questioned his monastic life as much as he embraced it. He yearned for silence as much as he enjoyed being in fraternity. In some ways, he basked in his celebrity as much as he sought humility. He was always discerning. He was a man of many contradictions, which is why I have always been drawn to him. Over time, he realized that his soul "gradually became in harmony with itself."

Take a moment and think about that. Isn't that a beautiful expression? Is *your* soul in harmony with *itself*?

Merton puts forth the assertion that we are *called to the true self*—not the person we think we want to be, not the person others want us to be, but the person God is calling us to be. He argues that there will *always* be an internal struggle, until we surrender to our true selves. And though they may never quite get there, servant leaders follow the journey to their true selves while working to help others discern their *own* true selves.

Part of finding the true self is confronting the false self. The false self is that person we wish to present to the world. It's the labels we put on ourselves. It's how we introduce ourselves: "Hi, I'm Bill, Senior Vice President." It's also how we analyze constraints; for example, "If I am good-looking, I will be more likable." "If I have a lot of money, I will be viewed as successful." Ego is just one of the things that challenge us while we become our true selves.

Both discernment and self-discovery are critical self-assessment tools for the servant leader. How can we persuade unless we are convinced ourselves? How can we have foresight unless we reflect and look back? How can we commit to the growth of others unless we have grown from within? How do we accomplish more by leveraging the organization's belief system?

My father leveraged his beliefs—he leveraged his empathy, care, compassion, and concern. He leveraged the heart and spirituality of our company in all that we did. Our firm's affordable housing practice was nationally recognized by syndicators, developers, housing authorities, lenders, and community development corporations. Housing provides shelter and a roof over a family's head. But it does *much* more than that. It provides a safe environment and a place to call home. It offers dignity and a sense of belonging. And if we are unable to provide affordable housing to our families, it jeopardizes our ability to provide access to childcare, job training, education, and even medical treatment.

It's about community-building. It's incredibly satisfying, knowing that through our work we contribute to new, affordable housing getting built and existing housing stock being preserved.

Our other large practice niche was in the not-for-profit sector. Running a not-for-profit has never been easy. We worked with over five hundred human service providers in Boston, in New England, and around the country. From substance abuse to youth services, from homelessness to elder services, from health education to working with organizations that assist families with developmental disabilities, this work became a significant part of our platform and voice as a mission-driven organization. The work only gets done in the way it gets done because it was managed by servant leaders and servant leaders in the making.

My dad had a vision, and he executed that vision as a humble servant. He knew how to push, and he knew how to pull, and he did both gently and with respect, grounded in trust and often with just a handshake. And all of this leads to new ideas, rapid innovation, a better organization, high-performing team members, and more engaged clients. It's a lesson in which *everybody* wins.

Regrets, I've Had a Few

"Step right up, folks," shouts the carnival barker. "Everyone's a winner."

This just might be the secret to living a fuller life.

I'm going to offer you some of the best advice that you might ever hear in your lifetime. And just like the carnival barker, these ideas compete every day with other appealing and tempting distractions and diversions.

As a Catholic deacon, I've spent lots of time with lots of people who had weeks, days—even hours—to live. They talked; I listened. One day, we are young and invincible with all our hopes and dreams within grasp, and for so many, each day, that distant horizon of our own mortality has a way of finding us with its cold indifference. Most of us don't really think about death until we have to.

There is something both haunting and hypnotic about chatting it up with someone who is knowingly on their own death watch, looking into a very long, unknown shadow. There is also something humbling, and a sense of privilege, in being with someone who is about to pass and having some influence over their death experience. Just as people live in different ways, people die in different ways.

In my final year of the diaconate program, I was assigned to the chaplain's office at MGH as part of a practicum semester. It was a spiritual residency at one of the world's top hospitals. It was also a time in my life that I look back on with a wide grin, having learned so much, finding emotions that I didn't know too well, and having had the depths of my heart set aflame on many occasions. Who would have guessed that seven years later my dad would be visited by a chaplain in the same hospital, in the same ICU that I had visited many times before as a volunteer?

Often, I was assigned to a series of floors in a particular building—Blake, Gray, Bigelow, Ellison, or Bullfinch. If I weren't busy—and that wasn't too often—I would simply explore the hospital campus . . . a labyrinth of underground tunnels, a beautiful chapel . . . and the infamous Ether Dome, a surgical amphitheater and site of the first public surgery using anesthetic (ether), and currently home to an Egyptian mummy.

Aside from an assigned list of patient visits, I would sometimes get intel at the nurse's station about a patient not on the list who really needed a visit. It was often in *those* visits where I found the limits of our humanity looking for avenues of closure.

I knocked on Murray's door and very much respected the threshold, not crossing it until I was invited in.

"Hi Murray, I'm Kevin, one of the volunteers at the chaplain's office. I thought I would stop in and see how you were doing."

"What do you mean you're a volunteer, they don't pay you?" Murray asked in a slow-paced and weak voice.

"No, they don't pay me, but I would have been happy to pay the hospital for the amount of grace I've found here. I'm in the diaconate program at St. John's Seminary."

"So, you're Catholic?"

"Yes, sir, I'm Catholic and I pray to be ordained in about a year."

"Good for you, your parents gave you faith, that's nice. I'm a Jew. What am I going to do with a Catholic deacon?"

"No idea, Murray, but neither one of us will find out unless you invite me in!"

"Come in, come, don't just stand there, we're both burning daylight. I think the last time I talked to a Catholic chaplain was in the war. Do you know if they called my daughter?"

"I want to hear all about the war, and I will ask the nurse about your daughter before I go."

I pulled a chair up; I felt welcomed. Murray was in a double room but the bed nearest the window was empty. He told me that he had a blood disease but didn't get any more particular. He used no medical terminology but told me quite a few times that he had been in and out of the hospital over the past few months.

"They don't give me much time. They told me I had a few months left a few months ago," he emphasized. "Do you know if they called my daughter?"

"I don't know, but I can try to find out," I promised Murray.

"My son is in Colorado. All he does is work. Never had time for his family . . . just like me, I guess. I hardly know his kids. But he calls, he does what he can. Colorado is far, he just built a new house, he invited me . . . but I don't think that's happening. He knows I'm sick but it's a long plane ride."

"I was in Colorado Springs, once; it was very nice. Is your wife still alive?"

"She died about ten years ago, love of my life. We were made for each other. Good mother, too. She did a lot of volunteer work. Do you know if they called my daughter?"

"Tell me about your daughter, what's her name? Where does she live? I'll find out for you."

"Emily, she's a good girl. I haven't seen her for a long time. She stays in touch with my son, I think. She's gay, you know. The two of them live together now. It wasn't my thing, I told her that . . . probably said too much, as I think about it now. She's a good girl, works at a bank, and has a dog, my son said. I probably said too much, but *she* did, too . . . it *wasn't* just me. I think she would come if they called her. Yeah, I probably said too much. Did they call her yet?"

Murray and I talked for hours. He liked cribbage, and though we didn't play that day—we didn't have a board—we talked about some of our best hands. He pulled me in with a couple of off-color jokes, each of which I had heard before. Murray asked me to hold his hand, which I was happy to do, and asked me what prayers I would say if he were Catholic. I told him that I would offer to pray the rosary with him, and he told me to do that and he would listen.

"In the name of the Father, and of the Son, and of the Holy Spirit," I began.

The nurses knew nothing about Murray's daughter. That seemed off to me. I went back to check in on him a couple of days later. Murray had died, and I don't know if he ever talked to her.

Regrets come in all shapes and sizes.

Just like Murray, as people reflect on their lives, I've learned that most people do have some regrets when they die. And those regrets, generally, end up in one or more of three buckets: (1) the regret of family disharmony; (2) the regret of a lack of travel and adventure; and (3) the regret of legacy and making a difference.

Other people's experiences may be different. This is just my impression, based on familiarity with the good people I got to know and listen to in their homes, in a hospital, in a rehab or, sometimes, in hospice. And, of course, this list doesn't include those things that we *can't* control like, "I'm not going to live long enough to walk my daughter down the aisle on her wedding day." That's a tough one, like so many other uncontrollable things that cause us suffering.

But what *can* we control?

First, the regret of family disharmony. Remember that time you had the big blowout with your brother or sister, mom or dad, cousin or uncle, or dear friend? It may have been over a special piece of mom's jewelry, the family business, the family home, a big fence between properties, a girl, a boy, money, someone getting pushed in the kitchen, the drunken comment made at the Thanksgiving table. But whatever it was, things were never the same after it happened. Murray knew this firsthand.

And though we drew some type of line in the sand when we were healthy—and though we think it's the other person who drew that line—it hurts even *more* when we are about to die. Years get lost, maybe even decades.

Yes, decades. And if we are not *in* one of those families, we *know* one of those families. There are unspoken words of lost time, feelings, expressions, hugs—people carry *profound* regrets with them.

Second is the regret of travel and adventure. There was always the good intention to see faraway lands, join the Peace Corps, walk in Jesus's footsteps in Galilee, kiss the Blarney Stone, go hiking in Iceland, bike through Tuscany—but it never happened. Sometimes we play it safe, taking the annual weekend trip to Woodstock, Catalina Island, or Branson, *repeatedly*.

We figure we'll take those big trips starting next year. We will have time to climb Kilimanjaro, hike El Camino de Santiago, see the Northern Lights, and the Great Pyramid at Giza. Or, more simply, we plan to eat Chicago-style pizza *in Chicago*. Somewhere along the way, we realize that we played it safe and became a creature of habit and never saw too much of anything.

Each of us has limitations, big and small. If we are allergic to gluten, we might not find the perfect pizza in Chicago. If we are in a wheelchair, we might not climb Everest. If we have no disposable income, a vacation to Paris may not be possible. If we struggle with anxiety, we might not give ourselves permission to get on a plane. However, by embracing our limitations, finding meaning in them, and building resilience as a result of them, we unlock all the adventures life has to offer.

Victor Frankl was an American neurologist, psychiatrist, philosopher, author, and Holocaust survivor, who once wrote, "Everything can be taken from a man but one thing: the last of the human freedoms—to choose one's attitude in any given set of circumstances, to choose one's own way." So, while Sigmund Freud believed that humans are motivated by their desire for pleasure, Frankl believed that life's purpose was not found in life's bounty, but rather from its struggles and limitations.

If finances or other personal limitations prevent you from going to Paris, how about taking a French wine class at your local center for adult education? And if that's not possible, how about getting dressed up, taking an online cooking class, and learning how to make Beef Bourguignon, and spending a late night in front of the television watching *Julie and Julia*, starring Meryl Streep and Amy Adams? Adams's character embarked on a project to prepare all 524 recipes of Julia Child's cookbook, *Mastering the Art of French Cooking*. And intertwined with the backstory is the tale of how Julia Child herself overcame her own limitations through passion, fearlessness, and butter . . . lots and lots of butter.

Last comes leaving a legacy and making a difference. It's the goal ring that so often goes unattained. Sure, most of us will never cure ALS or cancer. But most of us are content to look no further than our own backyards for something to do and engage in. Occasionally, we write a check to make ourselves feel good. But did we make a difference? *Really?* Did we get involved in something bigger than ourselves? Did we sweat over it? Did we lose sleep trying to figure it out? *Really?* Many people with only a few breaths remaining will say, "No, I didn't, and I *really* wish I had."

"What if?" is a tough question that we sometimes ask ourselves. No matter how happy we are with our lives, we can't help but wonder what else could have been. Most people would not have climbed Kilimanjaro under any circumstances. But they might still ask themselves, what if I had eaten better? What if I had taken piano lessons? What if I had sung in the choir? What if I had followed my calling? What if I had had kids? What if I had had *more* kids? What if I had spent more time with my parents? What if I had not been so critical of how others chose to live their lives? What if I had gotten involved with my church or temple or mosque?

To the best of my knowledge, my dad died happy and with few to no regrets. I'm sure he wished he could have lived another dozen years. I'm sure he wished his parents had lived longer. Maybe he wished he had learned to ride a bike. But, in the life he lived, in the life *he* could control, in the time *he* was allotted, he got along with everyone, he had deep relationships, he traveled the world, and went to every place he ever wanted to go, plus lots of places he had never heard of, and he made a difference. He gave of himself every day in simple and practical ways.

Dying without regrets? Give *me* a piece of that! In a quote that's often attributed to Buddha, we are reminded, "The trouble is, you think you have time." Life is short and we must make good use of it. There may be no "later."

In one of his final expressions of peace before the ventilation mask was placed on his thin face for the last time, he said, "We had a *really* good run."

And so, the best advice I could ever give to you—guaranteed or your money back—is for you to have your *own* really good run for as long as you can, and to not let anyone or anything stand in your way.

Get along with your family and friends. Accept them for who they are. Show up for the holidays. Every once in a while, feel free to bite your tongue.

Love your sons- and daughters-in-law. Don't be too quick to hire a lawyer; it never ends well for anyone. Have one karaoke song in your back pocket that you can kill. Use sunscreen.

Those little walls you've built up through the years with some people? Be merciful, and tear them down.

Go places. See things. Don't be a creature of habit. Float in the Dead Sea, take in the running of the bulls in Spain, attend the Russian ballet, find the girl from Ipanema. A few years back, when I was kicking around a soccer ball at *that* Brazilian beach at dusk with friends, I learned, believe it or not, that today "the girl" is in her mid-seventies and a grandmother.

Yeah, we *can't* afford to do *all* of them—but take in *something*, even *one* thing, and bask in repeating the stories for the rest of your life. Find ways around your limitations. And, most of all, make a difference in the lives of others. Get out in the world and make it better and stronger. Get outside of your white picket fence, leave the leaf-raking until next weekend, and bang a hammer for Habitat for Humanity, or register to coach a child with Down syndrome for the Special Olympics. Pick a social justice issue, like housing, immigration, poverty, or some other charitable work that causes your heart to skip a beat for all the right reasons, and double down on it.

And, when the sun sets, when the Angel of Death sets out to call on you, I promise you that this will be one of the best lessons you could have received in a hundred lifetimes.

"Come in a *little* closer, and I will tell you a secret," says the carnival barker. And you know what? Not only will these secrets have been a way to die without regrets, but maybe, along the way, you will have found the lesson of the meaning of your own life.

Lord Have Mercy

I can't remember one time that my father forgave me. Not even one.

But I'm not about to paint a terrible picture of an unforgiving father. It was just the opposite. My dad had this way about him: he never allowed a situation to escalate to the point of someone needing forgiveness.

He was a master of moving the pieces before a matter needed to be defused. He knew how to focus on matters of agreement rather than on matters of disagreement. And isn't that disarming? Isn't that a change in mindset? I have tried to emulate that lesson in my own life. It's not about flattery; it's about forcing collaboration and finding common ground.

Now here's a good example of art versus science. The science of forgiveness goes something like this:

"I'm sorry," he said.
"I forgive you," she responded.

And then ideally, "I love you," they both interrupted.

But often, life gets in the way, and it plays out *more like this*:

"When are you going to realize that you caused this?" he or she said. "Seriously, this has been building since Wednesday."

"Fine, we'll do it your way, have fun at the birthday party, I'm going to [*fill in the blank*]."

The blank might be play golf, go shopping with my sister, work in the yard, or catch up on some sleep.

It does not matter who it is; it could be a spouse, parent, son or daughter, sibling, or good friend, even a coworker. But the conflict between them, or the tension, just sits there . . . and sits there . . . and sits there some more. Sometimes for hours. Sometimes for weeks.

Sometimes a lot longer. Sometimes decades.

But the art of forgiveness is found in the story of the Prodigal Son.

The son comes home after having made many mistakes. He was wasteful and extravagant and returns home empty-handed. But his dad accepts him back, no questions asked. The reunion is a celebration. "But now we must celebrate and rejoice, because your brother was dead and has come to life again; he was lost and has been found." (Luke 15:32)

It's the same in our relationship with God. We often squander the grace provided to us for other types of worldly treasures that soon turn out to be worthless. We then fall back and are welcomed into the arms of grace over and over again. And it is by *this* grace that we are saved.

My dad was a simple guy. He was never about the drama. There was nothing dark about him. For all he achieved, he lived a very uncomplicated life. He was never the guy who needed to make a point, no matter how subtle. It just *wasn't worth it* to him. "Life's too short," he would remind me.

Sometimes we make our lives dramatic. Some of us are wired with extreme emotions which manifest into constant crises.

Imagine if we could all bypass making the argument. Imagine if we could intervene before the problem arises. We often wash our hands before we eat so we don't get sick later. And yet, in relationships, we often wash our hands clean when we've had enough.

My father was the master of forgiveness because you never knew you needed it.

Forgiveness is one of the toughest things that we do in our lives. The inability to forgive is part of our unfinished business that stays with us when we go to bed at night . . . night after night. When we can't let go of the past, it's impossible to love in the present. Forgiveness doesn't mean forgetting or letting someone off the hook, and it doesn't mean excusing or condoning bad things or unkind actions. You can forgive someone and still testify against them in court, if necessary. It is always still important to do the right thing.

Yes, some things are unforgivable. Cheating. Domestic violence. Murder.

Or are they?

I know a person who has forgiven the person who shot and killed her son. She visited him in prison, and she told him that she forgave him. I know a person who has forgiven the person who raped her. I know a person who has forgiven the person who infected him with HIV. If these people can forgive, can *we* forgive those others who trespass against *us*?

I don't know who said it, but I have heard several times the old expression, "Holding onto anger or resentment is like drinking poison and expecting the other person to die." Anger takes hold of us; it takes us hostage in many ways. When we are alone, we talk the matter over and over with ourselves to the point that we think we're going crazy. I've done that . . . and done that . . . and done that some more.

Forgiveness transforms anger into something bigger, far more powerful, and productive. It offers us peace and healing and some type of inner freedom. Imagine what that can do for our health. Depression, anxiety, stress, fear, and high blood pressure are but a short list of tangible ways anger takes its physical and emotional toll.

"But you don't understand my situation," you might say. I agree. Schoolyard bullies, psycho exes, alcoholism, sexual abuse, lousy childhoods . . . the list of possible hurts is endless.

It's easy to say, "Let it go." I get it.

When my dad died, I remembered who didn't come to the wake or funeral. I was hurt by the people who didn't check in to see how it was going. I was hurt by the seemingly insensitive things that people *did* say: "He's in a better place." "Everything happens for a reason." "I thought you would be over it by now." But what's the point of carrying that baggage? It gets heavier the longer you hold onto it. At some point, it gets so heavy you have to put it down.

The challenge for all of us is how we not only survive our hurts but how we become the lead in our own stories. Let's agree, scars hurt. Forgiveness allows us to free ourselves *from* them and grow *because* of them. It liberates us and brings peace. And perhaps the biggest benefit of all is that forgiveness allows us to open our hearts to both live and love again.

Never Stop Holding Hands

My mom and dad met in Southie when they were both thirteen. They were part of the same friend group that hung on the corner together. As the old Dean Martin song goes, "Standing on the corner watching all the girls, watching all the girls, watching all the girls go by." My folks were together for close to sixty-six years, soulmates by any definition.

Many people who knew my parents said they were on a forever honeymoon. I still often hear, "They were always together; they were tied at the hip." And they were, and that's *just* the way they liked it.

Sometimes, marriages get into trouble when the marriage turns into a business—the business of paying the bills, working in the yard, shopping for food, taking care of the kids, getting kids to school, cleaning the house, and balancing careers. Of course, this is *very* real stuff. The "work of marriage" *must* get done. But we can get lost in the chores and minutiae, too, and that's when a subtle emotional distance creeps in. And once it creeps in, it becomes like a window draft on the coldest of New England days.

I'm hardly a marriage counselor, but as a deacon I am often in the informal—but still very holy—space of spouses looking for guidance and perspective, or maybe just needing someone to nod their heads without word or judgment. That might happen formally or informally, before Mass in a quiet pew, at the back of church, or in the supermarket. I've even had some unusual conversations in well-appointed funeral parlors. Parishioners know that I'm married and have four kids, and Lisa and I balance two careers and a lot of volunteer work. This means I can relate to parishioners as a spouse, more so than a priest could.

"My husband drinks too much."

"My wife doesn't pay any attention to me."

"My wife takes care of her parents; there's never any time for us."

"My husband works, plays golf with his friends, and watches football; what should I do?"

"For all the reasons why we got married in the first place, all of those qualities seem to have disappeared."

Marriage is not easy.

My parents invested in their marriage. They *always* found time for each other. That's the lesson.

On some cold winter Sundays, my mom and dad would go to church and walk around Copley Place in Boston, a large indoor mall with lots of shops and restaurants. After a minor heart attack and two stents, a dozen or so years ago, my dad liked to walk as much as he could. They would browse through the bookstore, window shop, and have coffee. They always had a book with them. My mom kept them tidily stashed in one of her enormous pocketbooks. If their adventure took them into Boston in the afternoon, they would sink into the couch by the fireplace, in a well-appointed Boston hotel lobby, read their books, enjoy a glass of wine, and just read and people-watch. Lisa and I have picked up the habit. It feels like a mini-vacation without the bill at checkout.

On Friday nights, my parents would often find themselves at the movies and out for a pizza. My mother would call me earlier in the day and ask me if Lisa and I had seen this or that, or would ask if I knew why a movie had an R-rating.

A beautiful spring weekday might find them playing hooky from work. On the right kind of day, my mom would make lunch, and they would go to Boston's Public Garden and have a picnic and people-watch. My dad had an old radio that he brought along because they both enjoyed listening to the Red Sox.

Again, he was from another era. They both were.

They would ride the Swan Boats—a short boat ride around the Public Garden lagoon—and my dad would sometimes buy an entire school field trip of kids bags of peanuts to eat or toss to the ducks. The day would usually end with a stroll on Charles Street and dinner.

The fall would find my folks on a train to New York. Always a train, never a plane. My dad figured by the time you go to Boston's Logan Airport, go through security, take the short flight, and then a taxi to the hotel, the Amtrak Acela could do it in the same amount of time in a far more relaxed manner. Walk on, read, eat, walk off. And over the course of two to three days, they would walk and walk and walk, visit a museum or two, attend a Broadway show, go to dinner, and attend Mass at St. Patrick's Cathedral. When my kids were younger, one of them would stow away, and the trip might include a visit to see Santa at Macy's or shop at FAO Schwartz or the American Girl Doll store. Sometimes my parents went with friends, but no matter what, it was one of their annual journeys.

And nothing exemplified that honeymoon attitude more than their annual trip to Walt Disney World in Florida. We had taken many trips to Disney as a family, but my parents still took those trips even when we weren't freeloading. They did it every year, the week before Thanksgiving, for as long as I can remember. They would always stay at Disney's Saratoga Springs Resort & Spa, which was an easy walk to Downtown Disney. My mother enjoyed the animals at Animal Kingdom, my dad enjoyed the Haunted House at the Magic Kingdom, and they both enjoyed Ellen's Energy Adventure dinosaur ride at Epcot, which I hear has closed. My mother never really learned how to use her camera phone, and I would often get pictures of a foot or a chair or a door that I think were supposed to be pictures of their trip. They had their favorite restaurants and shows, and always remembered the waitstaffs' names. And the waitstaff always remembered my parents' names and that my mom has celiac disease, an allergy to "everything gluten." Yum.

My mom protected my dad vigorously. She gave him his pills each morning, something she did for over twenty-five years. He didn't take much—a daily aspirin and a blood thinner that he was prescribed after his mild heart attack in his late sixties.

At work, she would make his lunch. It wasn't a family business, but it *was* a family affair.

My mom monitored my dad's diet very carefully. She would only cook beef once a week; she rarely bought cold cuts or ice cream. She reminded him that salami wasn't good for you, no matter how little you ate. She maintained that part of her contribution to their marriage was keeping my dad healthy. And she did.

My parents' marriage worked because it was a partnership. My dad never walked in front of my mom, and my mom never walked behind my dad. My dad had a beautiful picture of him and my mom in his office. It was taken many years ago aboard the Orient Express. When first-time visitors would come into my dad's office, he often pointed to the photo and exclaimed in delight, "How lucky am I!"

If you read a marriage self-help book—and there are tons of them—we get lots of good ideas on what makes a happy marriage: love, forgiveness, patience, good communication, commitment, time together. There are endless suggestions. Perhaps part of our responsibility as a spouse is to help our partner get to Heaven. And while we ponder that, here are two simpler thoughts.

My mom and dad never stopped holding hands. All those trips, all those walks, so many of their photos, they were *always* holding hands. When they went to bed at night, they fell asleep holding hands. Show me a couple who is holding hands when they go to bed at night, and I'll show you a couple who doesn't need marriage advice. They've figured all that *other* stuff out.

And the other? My mom and dad had their song, "Could I Have This Dance" by Anne Murray. Love can be shown in many ways other than saying it. My mom and dad loved to dance, from "The Twist" to "The Tennessee Waltz." Fast, slow—it didn't matter; they enjoyed the dance and the songs that were playing, and they swayed to the music and fell in love over and over again.

Health Is Wealth

How many times have we heard the simple expression, "Health is wealth"? Though it sounds novel, and though we've heard it frequently, it is something my dad reminded us of many times through the years—most particularly during his ICU stay, where he wrote it many times in his hospital journal.

Admit it. We take our health for granted, especially when we have it. And when we don't, it sometimes takes over our lives. Even the *possibility* of illness can wreak havoc on us. Many of us have lost sleep over what we thought was a small lump that turned out to be a big pimple, or a pain in our left arm. We thought it might be the onset of a heart attack, but it turned out to be a strain from working in the yard or taking out the trash.

Google "headache causes." From the results, you can choose between stress and hangover to stroke, concussion, meningitis, dental problems, brain tumor . . . or maybe, simply, you skipped lunch and you're suffering the consequences.

Often, it's *not* as bad as you think it is.

When my dad first started getting weaker, no one symptom was predominant. He was losing weight, but we knew that older people sometimes have less of an appetite. His hands bothered him, but he had been playing a fair amount of golf for over thirty-five years and some arthritis had crept in. His legs felt weak, but he thought it might be vascular.

It's important that we listen to our bodies and what they tell us. If you Google "muscle weakness," you can choose from causes like West Nile virus, herniated disk, various thyroid conditions, too much exercise, electrolyte imbalances, and many neurological disorders, from Parkinson's to multiple sclerosis (MS)—to, of course, ALS.

In the beginning, we were sure it was a herniated disc, because basic x-rays supported that practical diagnosis. In the end, as crazy as it sounds, I prayed my dad had many *other* diseases, because I knew that any one of them could be managed better and longer than ALS.

Sometimes it *can* be worse than you think it is.

I have an appreciation for hospitals. Having performed my diaconate practicum at MGH, it is hard for me to walk or ride by a hospital without looking up and taking pause, thinking what might be happening inside those big buildings on that day—perhaps a heart attack, stroke, chemo, an MRI, stress test, a gunshot wound, or suicide attempt. And there are so many miracles that also happen in the operating room, family waiting room, and maternity ward—maybe even twins. Good news and bad news abound.

My dad played sports from an early age and ate healthy, more or less—my mother made sure of it, despite some mild flirtation with pepperoni, salami, and an occasional Saturday night fried bologna and french fries, hot from the skillet. His blood pressure was better than perfect, and his cholesterol was better than mine.

When he was young, my father played football, and many organized sports in boarding school. He then moved to handball at the L Street Bathhouse, more formally known as the Curley Community Center.

Learning how to play handball was a rite of passage, growing up in Southie. Along the way, there were fewer and fewer handball players, and many Southie guys, including my dad, turned to racquetball at the Boston Athletic Club. And though racquetball kept his heart pumping, it is intense. Players are darting and racing, making sudden twists and turns and starts and stops near one another. Racquets are swung forcefully and mercilessly as players work hard to hit the tiny rubber ball.

When my mom and dad bought their Cape Cod house, my dad gave up racquetball and took up golf and walking. In hindsight, it seemed age-appropriate. He walked the beach in Southie to Castle Island. He walked the beach in Brewster. He walked with my mom and he walked alone, and he walked the aisles in the supermarket while my mom shopped. On a snowy day, I might call my mom to check in and say, "Where's Dad?" It was not unusual for her to respond, "He went to Home Depot, to do his walk."

I have not yet moved to more age-appropriate activities. I'm a triathlete and generally indulge in a half-dozen or more races between June and September. I like moving and swallowing the fresh air. I enjoy the sun on my face, and the wind at my back. I revel in the hot shower after the cold run and the cold shower after the hot bike ride. I belong to a US Masters swim club, and the water offers both adrenaline and a sense of tranquility in the laps. I bask in the hard work, consistency, discipline, and required mental toughness. It's my way of acknowledging that health is wealth, and I relish in sharing a meal with other athletes and hearing how they deftly manage a jam-packed schedule, and work through obstacles and adversity. We share health and nutrition tips, and lessons learned. For now, I continue to ignore articles that talk about how clinical data suggests how too much intense exercise can lead to ALS, and how triathletes are overrepresented in a population of patients with ALS.

No matter how much success, money, or fame we may enjoy, it's useless without good health. When we are young, we can push our bodies to the limit day after day, with few repercussions. We think we are invincible. As we grow older, too much partying, boozing, smoking, vaping, and eating fast food takes a toll.

My dad wanted to be healthy, and he worked at it.

Exercise and eat well. But it doesn't stop there. My dad had the right attitude. He didn't take things personally. He believed in "live and let live." He was tolerant. He laughed out loud a lot. He was curious. He slept well.

Aging is inevitable. Sagging and wrinkles are going to set in. We can find beauty in aging and declining health. We learn not to waste time. And when we begin to accept our limitations, grace and wisdom set in. It's a good lesson.

"The first wealth is health," American philosopher Ralph Waldo Emerson wrote in 1860.

And though Kevin Martin agreed with Emerson, it was no longer meant to be. Despite a clean-living lifestyle, sometimes plain, old bad luck catches up with us, and all we can do is take God's hand and do our best to make something splendid grow from it.

Let Me Understand This: The Devil Is in the Details

"Mr. Martin, we want to update you on what we think is going on at this point," said the doctor. "You aspirated at home. You *do* have an infection, and though we don't see any pneumonia, we are treating you for pneumonia just so we stay ahead of it. Pneumonia is a common side effect of aspiration," he went on to say.

Though I had heard the word "aspiration" before, I had never quite understood what it really meant. This is a condition where pneumonia develops after you've inhaled bacteria (through food, drink, saliva, or vomit) into your lungs. Too much liquid in your lungs can also result in pulmonary edema, which puts a strain on your lungs.

"I understand. How long will I be here?" my dad asked in a raspy voice, an hour or so after his intubation tube had been removed.

"Well, that's still unclear," the doctor said. "We are trying to get the infection under control. But even if we do," he went on to say, "ALS is still in the background. That's what's making this more complicated."

"So, this is all about the ALS?" my dad asked in a curious way. It is interesting that my dad referred to it as "the ALS" and not "my ALS." One word can make a difference. It makes the disease accessible. Unknowingly, from the depths of his heart, it allowed him to send out heartfelt compassion to those with the same illness. When it's "my ALS" or "my cancer," it isolates us from the care of others, and we stand alone in it.

"I'm afraid so."

"I don't think I fully realized that. What does that mean?" my dad asked.

"Our concern is that even if we get you home, this is likely to happen again."

They had this conversation at the hospital. But we knew something was wrong earlier that night, when Lisa and I brought dinner to them at my mother's house. My mom seemed to know that *something* wasn't quite right and asked us to come in.

My dad appeared confused. He was shaking. He seemed weak.

As we would learn later, his carbon dioxide levels had likely been rising for days, maybe even weeks.

"So, let me make sure I understand. This is more about the ALS than anything?" he asked again.

"That's right," repeated the doctor.

"And if I go home, this is likely to happen again?"

"Yes."

"And because my respiratory system is getting weaker, I will need a full-time ventilator?"

"That's right."

"Well, it would seem I should want to try that first, and we can always make a different decision later?" Analyzing data always meant evaluating alternatives.

"True."

"Can I still get out of the house and go to work?"

"That's likely not going to be practical. The machine is big, like the one next to you."

"Oh, I didn't know it was that big," my dad said as he glanced to his right. "How would I eat, then, if I always have a breathing mask on?"

"We would put a port in your stomach for a feeding tube, and we would put a full-time trach in your throat so you could speak. But over time, the ALS will likely take away your ability to talk."

"I understand. This is all different than I thought. OK, I understand. This is actually . . . this is actually . . . the end . . . the end of the road," my dad stuttered with a heavy sigh.

Tears filled the room. They were quiet tears, for nobody wanted to add to the drama that was unfolding before us.

Though many people suffering with ALS live two to five years, my father was hit with respiratory issues early on. Air hunger. Fatigue. Early morning headache. Insomnia. Difficulty lying flat. Most ALS deaths result from respiratory failure, and this seemed to be the path that we were speeding down *rapidly*.

"Kevin, we can do this," my mom cried out to my dad. "I will take care of you. You can't leave me. We can stay home; we can make this work."

"Claire, it doesn't work," my dad said as he shook his head. "It doesn't seem fair to me, and it *definitely* isn't fair to you. It's not a life."

"I can't live without you. Let's do this. It would be better for us to be together. It doesn't matter what we are doing, as long as we are together."

"Claire, listen to what the doctor is saying. I'm not going to get better. The ALS is in the background in all of this. Even if I get home, it's going to happen again, and it's getting more complicated."

"I know, I know, I know," my mom admitted.

My dad had a certain intellectual curiosity about so many things—sports, politics, the stock market. He liked the liveliness of debate, but his opinion was always grounded in research, analysis, conversations, and much attention to detail.

And so, my dad made the decision, after reviewing *all* the data, what made the most sense. Emotions aside, the data drove his decision. The decision was made to start palliative care, sign a DNR, and let nature begin to take its course.

Emotion is important. But the data told my father otherwise. The winter before my dad was diagnosed, I was accepted into Harvard's Data Analytics Program. I took a deferral, due to his illness. Data analysis is how good decisions are made. Without good data, bias, bad judgment, and personal preference can cause poor decision-making, even in making end-of-life decisions.

My dad and I had different management styles and approaches to life. We complemented each other well. I make many decisions based on intuition, on how I feel, on instinct. That's not how my dad operated. And that difference is what makes the world go round. But no matter what, we can't ignore the data.

Sometimes there can be a fine line between paying attention to detail and being practical. My dad knew that fine line well.

My dad was one of those "measure twice, cut once" guys. Not a bad lesson.

I Must Suffer More

Suffering is an expansive topic. One we spend a lifetime trying to figure out. And we never do.

Of all the hospital notes my father wrote to us, of all the conversations we had in the hospital, there was one series of notes that put me over the edge. They still do.

"I must suffer," he wrote to us repeatedly.

What was *that* about? Why would anybody *want* to suffer? Why would he not have just wanted to get better? What did he mean by *those* words?

And when we pushed the conversation, the next note would read, "I must suffer *more*."

My dad told us several times in the hospital that he had to suffer to get to Heaven. Was he confused? Was it all the medicine? Who was putting these crazy thoughts in his head?

As a deacon, I've studied suffering but mostly in the third-person, in trying to understand and rationalize it. I've visited dying patients in hospitals and hospices who have asked me, as clergy, "Why am I suffering?" or "Why is my mother or husband suffering?" Suffering is often discussed in the form of a question or a pondering, *rarely* as an affirmation, as in, "I *must* suffer."

My dad was practical, and analytical, and put pieces together. He connected the dots, and he *always* knew how to get from Point A to Point B, and so the lesson is worth unraveling.

Everyone suffers at some point, and we don't know why. *War and Peace* author Leo Tolstoy offered his thoughts on suffering: "Man cannot possess anything as long as he fears death. But to him who does not fear it, everything belongs. If there was no suffering, man would not know his limits, would not know himself."

It's one of life's greatest mysteries, why we suffer like we do, from childhood cancer, floods, and earthquakes. Mass shootings. Bad marriages. Unemployment. Families that don't speak to one another. Fatal car accidents. Addiction.

Sometimes our suffering results from unfulfilled desires. It causes us a quality of longing rather than being. We sometimes look into the lives of our friends and other family members, and we think their lives are somehow better . . . they just seem happier.

In some ways, we were *that* family. Lisa and I had a good marriage. We had good kids. We had good jobs. We volunteered for good causes. We were active in our church. We were happy. There was no baggage. We had never suffered through a tough time. "Life is good" was bigger than a t-shirt to us.

And then my dad got diagnosed with ALS. Everything changed. Suffering was no longer a concept, no longer something witnessed from a distance.

ALS turns the body against itself as the disease attacks nerve cells in the brain and spinal cord, leaving the brain unable to communicate with the body's muscles and causing them to waste away. Gradually, patients lose their ability to walk, move their arms, or eat. And talk. And breathe.

My father's faith was strong. My mom's faith *is* strong. She says it's not, but it is. She prays the rosary *every day*. She always has some type of novena going. She attends or watches Mass on television *every day*. We all just have different ways of expressing our faith.

My dad believed in the power of the cross. He believed that in order to fully align ourselves with Christ, some amount of suffering was part of the journey, of all our journeys.

Now, we don't all have to agree on this point. There is no effort on my behalf to sell you a bumper sticker that says, "Bring on the suffering." And yet, do we know of *anybody* who has ever died who has not endured some amount of suffering along life's journey? Maybe in the beginning, or the middle, or the end?

Suffering is an inevitable facet of life. And though we know it, we resist it. And here is what's at least interesting: if we can't agree on why suffering happens, or who or what causes it, maybe we can at least agree on our response to suffering. The Buddha taught that "behind the pain there is always something we are attached to." When we can free ourselves from attachment, the reward is freedom.

My dad suffered and never felt it should be someone else. He never asked, "Why me?" Maybe we did, but *never* him.

When my dad got diagnosed, he doubled down on his beliefs. He continued to offer care, compassion, patience, and love. He continued to take care of us when we thought we were taking care of him. He continued to go to work and engage with people. He continued to call his grandchildren and find out about their days and offer advice.

And so, while my dad got weaker, while he continued to suffer rapid weight loss because he could no longer swallow very well, he continued to participate and engage by going out for dinner, going on car rides . . . in many ways, he did it to take care of us, because although he had accepted where he was, we hadn't, and the night remained dark.

What my dad taught us is that suffering can be responded to with hope, grace, respect, and dignity. Maybe not at first, but maybe this is what can come out the other side of the tunnel. They say that the darkest part of the night is right before dawn, and I was finding that in my own faith crisis.

We get caught up in why God lets bad things happen. Even as a deacon, I sometimes continue to yell at God for what He let happen to my father, and why He didn't give this "one in a million guy" the miracle he deserved. We were mad at Him, or at least *I* was mad at Him.

Feel free to yell at God. God can take it. And in that anger, and in that tough conversation, feel God's arms come around you even tighter.

What I keep coming back to is that God isn't sitting upstairs acting as a puppet master, pulling the strings and making bad things happen because He is bored. "I haven't had much to do lately, how about a good pandemic to keep things interesting?" But when bad things do happen, when people do hurt, that is when He jumps in, that is when He comforts us, that is when He consoles us, that is when He envelops us with His love. We often find God in the rubble of our lives, helping us to rebuild amidst the ruins.

My dad knew he was dying. He knew he had a terminal disease. We knew, too—we just didn't know it was going to be *so* terminal so incredibly soon.

My dad knew that he had this wonderful life with little suffering, and so how was he supposed to get from this life to eternal life? How would this *very* practical guy analyze that data? "I must suffer." And how does he die and get to Heaven *faster*? "I must suffer *more*." It's an astonishingly practical and simple thought process.

Unless death is immediate, from a heart attack or some form of tragedy, in the last days or week of life, most people suffer in some way from pain, nausea, hallucinations, anxiety, or other symptoms that we can hardly imagine. Yes, some people die peacefully in their sleep. How beautiful. Maybe *their* suffering happened earlier in their lives or under different circumstances.

And so, my dad *participated* in his dying. He was mindful. And the more mindful we are throughout our lives, the less crowded are our deathbeds. "We were born to die," he reminded us. It was not until a couple of hours before his death that he began to receive palliative care to calm his fears, and to ease his breathing so that he could be taken off the ventilator—something he may not have even had access to, not long after, at the peak of the coronavirus pandemic.

My dad was anointed by his local pastor days before he died. He went to confession. He had an inner freedom. He was prayed over by Cardinal O'Malley. My dad's heart rate calmed itself from 171 to 88 beats per minute during those prayers. My dad was able to engage in those end-of-life rituals even more than we know.

What do we believe? More than trying to understand suffering, that's what this chapter asks of us. Both suffering and death recall our human condition and the brevity of our lives on earth. But for those who believe in God's love, none of this is final. We, too, shall be raised up. That's what my dad was indirectly asking his family. That's the lesson he was giving us.

Pre-COVID, on the most ordinary days, we would drop kids off at school, go to work, hit the gym, go grocery shopping, and clean our houses. Sometimes, if we're lucky, we take a vacation. And, if we are so fortunate, we have a family with which to share *all* of it. It's a big deal when we can move from these most ordinary and usual things to periods of suffering in some very outward way to some inward movement of our souls. When we can be raised up and move our souls on their journey, isn't that one of the most liberating and remarkable things that can happen during this lifetime?

There is no question that my dad was having inward movements of his soul during his final days. *His* soul was harmonizing with itself. Though his body may have been shutting down, his thoughts were vivid, beliefs clear, perspective dramatic, and his contemplative imagination articulate. He had deep faith already, but he went through a spiritual transformation during those five days ending September 10, 2019. Though my dad was wrapped in warm blankets, there was a certain nakedness to him.

Thankfully, most of us aren't facing end-of-life decisions today. And yet, we can all relate to the question, "Why is life *so* hard sometimes?" It is still so difficult to understand why, and yet life's events *cause* us to make choices.

Suffering *allows* us to make choices, and those choices enable us to continue our journey. Do I choose addiction or freedom? Do I choose rebellion or hope? Do I move in this direction or that direction? And those choices allow us to grow in the most magnificent ways.

At the end of the movie *Charlie Wilson's War*, the CIA agent who had been working with Tom Hanks's character, Congressman Wilson, to overthrow the Soviet occupation of Afghanistan, looks back on the operation and tells Charlie a story:

> There once was a Zen master who hears that a boy has been given a horse for his sixteenth birthday.
> "How wonderful!" the people shout.
> "We'll see," says the Zen master.
> Then the boy falls off his horse and breaks his leg.
> "How terrible!" the people cry.
> "We'll see," says the Zen master. Soon a war breaks out, and the boy is spared from service because of his broken leg.
> "How wonderful!" the people shout.
> "We'll see," says the Zen master.

Though we were praying for an ALS physical healing miracle, we didn't get it. As the Zen master taught, we usually don't have the perspective to understand the long-term significance of events that occur in our lives. We are quick to say whether something is good or bad. By remaining open to *other* ways, we learn to let go of our *immediate* wants. That's when we learn to give up control. That's where acceptance comes in; that's where faith does its very best work.

And so, although we were tremendously saddened by all that was unfolding before us, we were pleased by all that remained unfinished.

Dad with his mother, Peg. St. Joseph School for Boys, Wellesley. May Day, circa 1955.

Dad's father, Mitty. Early 1950's.

The Martin brothers, clockwise from top left: Tom, Jerry, Dad, Mike. Early 1950's.

Mom and Dad's wedding day. May 19, 1962.

All aboard the Orient Express. Mom and Dad, circa 1989.

Father and son. Ireland, circa 1992.

Savoring game night. Circa all the time.

The gang, clockwise from the top: me, Dad, Kevin, Meghan, Brian, Connor, Lisa, Mom. Greece, June 2018.

Mom and Dad. Mediterranean cruise, June 2018.

The last photo, holding hands, M&Ms on the go.
Cape Cod, Labor Day weekend 2019.

Dad, as he is always remembered. Venice, June 2018.

PART THREE

The Puzzle

"I'm working on a puzzle," said my father. "I finished one this morning, and I did one last night, which makes sense because I had another one this morning," he went on. "God keeps giving me puzzles, and when I finish one, He gives me another and another. And when I finish the last one, that's when the gates of Heaven will open for me. Mary said it would be Tuesday, I need to complete the last puzzle by Tuesday morning."

Sounds a little bizarre, I agree. There was a window, a very brief window when time stood still. And we basked in the light of the window.

The window opened when the intubation tube was pulled from my father's throat, and the window closed a few hours later when his carbon dioxide rose to such a dangerous level it required he be affixed to a ventilator, without which, we would soon come to learn, he could no longer live. And for this moment, despite being in the ICU, hooked up to a bunch of machines, Camelot continued to reign, and my father was clear-headed and conversational in his tone, confident and comfortable with his thoughts. Besides the puzzles, my dad watched and talked about the Red Sox, expressed concern over the stock market, and discussed how salami is not good for you.

And isn't that what life is all about? Not so much about the salami, but how we spend our lives working on a series of puzzles, unraveling the mysteries that life offers us. Whether we are a Montessori toddler building the pink tower, a teenager struggling with college choices, a young couple trying to figure out whether this is *the one*, or a senior coping with the loss of a spouse, life offers us all these pieces and challenges in different shapes and sizes that we spend a lifetime weaving together.

And we never quite get the last few pieces. Sometimes they fall into the couch cushion, sometimes they fall under the coffee table. And sometimes they are the pieces of our lives that remain unsettled.

The lesson is to solve the puzzles of our lives. And that takes prayer, reflection, self-awareness, and lots of courage.

My dad lived his life solving puzzles. In work—he didn't look at it as work—he enjoyed solving complex problems and asking others to be open to creative solutions and new ideas. At home, he liked *real* puzzles and spending time with family putting them together after Sunday dinner while watching the football game. In his charity work, he challenged others to find new ways to deliver mission.

What's the puzzle happening in *your* life today? What are you trying to figure out? Are you just completing a puzzle and moving on to a new one, or have you been stuck in the same puzzle for a while? Piece by piece, we often can't see what it's all about, but as more pieces get added, as we work hard to find the right fit, clarity follows.

Let's face it. Our lives are all very different, and our puzzles are all very different. Sometimes the pieces fit together perfectly, and sometimes they don't fit the way we think they should.

It takes patience. It takes *lots* of patience.

We build our lives just as we would build a puzzle. Piece by piece. And over time, the vibrancy of the puzzle—and our lives—emerges. And though I don't know what the puzzle was, my dad must have completed his last puzzle on time because he died on Tuesday morning, just like he told us he would.

A Bucket List

bucket list. *noun, informal.* a list of experiences one would like to have or accomplishments one aspires to in their lifetime. origin: from the phrase *kick the bucket.* From *American Heritage Dictionary Online.*

We all have a list of things we dream about doing. As children, we dream a lot about what we might do when we grow up.

Kids dream big. They want to travel the world, become president of the United States, an astronaut, a major league baseball player, or a movie star. And yet, how many of us follow our childhood dreams? Hats off to those who do, but regrettably, most don't.

Our dreams begin to fade as time passes and reality sets in. At what point do we acknowledge that we are not going to

Yale, or that we are not going to be the next American Idol or Supreme Court justice? And, yeah, there's a pretty good chance that you *just* might not win an Oscar for best screenplay.

Family, work, taking care of children, being a primary caregiver for a parent, money concerns—over time, they all seem to start creating boundaries, limits, and constraints. We leave parts of our lives until later—but later often comes far sooner than we ever could have expected, leaving a sense of incompleteness and unfinished business. Without even knowing it, we start to settle.

My father never used the expression *bucket list,* a term popularized by a movie of the same name starring Morgan Freeman—yet again—and Jack Nicholson. However, since he was a child, my dad always pursued his dreams *while* finding joy in the ordinary.

Some of our bucket lists might include adventure travel like swimming with the sharks in South Africa, scuba diving the Great Barrier Reef, strolling along the Great Wall of China, or following in the footsteps of Lewis and Clark. Let's face it, someone has to do it. For others, it's more of a romantic fantasy. Have you ever wanted to dance the polka at Oktoberfest, bicycle through Tuscany, bask in the Blue Lagoon in Iceland, or enjoy the sunset in Santorini? Imagine floating in the Dead Sea, playing soccer on the beach in Rio, reading a book under a cherry blossom tree in Japan, or meditating in a Buddhist monastery in Nepal? All these things are exhilarating and exciting, maybe also peaceful and calming.

Bucket lists also come in many shapes and sizes. Oftentimes, the entries include big travel or proud accomplishments such as writing a book, learning how to play the piano, growing a bonsai tree, or learning another language. Have you considered building your own kite, inventing something, performing a set at open mic night, or auditioning to be on *Jeopardy*? And don't forget killing that karaoke song.

Decades ago, my parents took one of those once-in-a-lifetime trips aboard the Orient Express, uncovering a timeless, hidden moving jewel. *Choo, choo, chug. Choo, choo, chug.* Elegant dining carriages, culinary sophistication, the resident pianist filling the air with sweet melodies. Cabins adorned with art deco details and polished cherry wood. My folks traveled from Venice to London with good friends, enjoying afternoon tea, admiring the passing scenery, and hearing stories of murder and intrigue.

Steve Martin has taught me comedy, a dream come true. Really. Well, kinda. About a year or so ago, I bought a subscription to the online classroom *MasterClass*. A master class is a class given to students by an expert in a certain discipline. Imagine learning filmmaking from Martin Scorsese, cooking from Gordon Ramsay, acting from Natalie Portman, photography from Annie Leibovitz, or singing from Christina Aguilera. It's about successful and inspiring people at the top of their game, teaching the secrets of their success. It's eLearning at its creative best. From my perspective, here's the head fake, intended or not. Along the way, after taking several classes—and each class has a dozen or so modules—you realize there are commonalities and underlying principles that you can apply to your own passion and journey.

So, what *is* the difference between kissing the Blarney Stone in County Cork, tasting fine bourbon at the Jim Beam Distillery along the Bourbon Trail in Kentucky, or, more simply, writing a beautiful song for a special someone? In order—very expensive, less expensive, no cost at all.

Is that the difference? Could it be *that* simple? How are they the same? What's the commonality? Maybe they're all things you've never done before. Maybe they're all things you've always wanted to do. Maybe they're all things that offer *deep* satisfaction and accomplishment for having done them. Maybe they're personal for all the right emotional, physical, or spiritual reasons. Maybe, mostly, they're all things you'll remember having done for the *rest of your life.*

Ah-ha!

Now imagine you're in a hospital bed. You're dying. You're connected to machines. The nurses are drawing blood every couple of hours. The heart monitor's beep-beep-beep prevents you from dozing. You've got your *own* journal. Right now, put down the book, find a pen, and write *that* list . . . a bucket list. What do you write?

Maybe, years ago, you would have put "take a cruise down the Danube" on your bucket list—but not today. Nobody puts "have a bunch of kids" on their early bucket list, but what could be more important now? In that bed, what would cause you remorse or regret? Never having loved? Not forgiving on the many occasions that you could have? Not having made a difference?

Everyone gets something different from the lesson, but no matter what we pull from it, it reminds us of our own mortality and that life is short—*very* short. Each year, each of us passes over our death day. *Memento Mori.* Why wait to live our best life? Why wait to become more fully alive? Imagine if we could truly experience each breath as if we thought it were our last.

Imagine if we entered each moment, each conversation, and each lovemaking as though there may never be another.

And in that reflection, it brings us back to our childhoods with all our hopes and dreams—and it hopefully challenges us to take another bite at the apple. *Carpe diem.* It causes us to change our optics in some way. Maybe it even causes us to enable the dreams of others.

And as opposed to looking at family and work and taking care of elderly parents as holding us back in some way, we realize that *all* of it is part of who we are and is an important part of *our* journey, *and* theirs.

We can embrace it, find gratitude in it, and go further. We can find joy in it.

Joy

People have often told me that my father had a certain twinkle in his eye, a certain rhythm to his step, a certain something special that emanated from him. It was more than simply being a nice, modest guy. He had that "it" factor, a certain *je ne sais quoi*.

What was it? In some mystical way, I guess it was his aura. But it goes *far* deeper and wider than that.

There could be a thousand people in the room, but when my dad's eyes engaged you for conversation, he was locked in and you had him—*all* of him. You had every bit of him for as long as you wanted. He *never* looked over your shoulder, scoping out his next greeting opportunity.

My father was a believer. My father had a gladness about him—that is what you saw on his face. He had joy in his heart. "Joy is different than happiness," he would say. "Joy lasts, happiness doesn't."

And for the most part, his remarks on the subject never went much deeper than that. He spoke concisely—short and to the point. When I was younger, I never thought too much about it. It was usually said in the context of witnessing an event or occurrence, or in response to some type of kitchen table discussion.

The lesson is simple.

We find happiness in so many things and in so many ways. On a warm summer's Cape Cod night, I enjoy nothing more than two big scoops of chocolate chip ice cream in a sugar cone. I delight in a weeklong trip to Walt Disney World with my family, nothing bringing me more satisfaction than having us all together, enjoying some old-fashioned fun. Pizza, a good book, and binge-watching *The Crown* on a Friday night? That's my idea of a good time. All these things bring me happiness.

And yet each of these happy things is fleeting. Often, by the last spoonful, I regret having had the ice cream. The trip leaves beautiful memories, but a certain melancholy kicks in on the flight home.

"Back to reality" is a feeling most of us have experienced. And that last chapter of a special book sometimes leaves us wanting more.

Happiness is a *temporary* state. Nobody knows how short-lived happiness can be than the person who seeks the fountain of youth and undergoes the $25,000 facelift. Just ask them in ten years! Their happiness erodes at the rate of about $2,500 per year. Time catches up with us no matter how big our checkbook, or how far back we pull our sagging jowls.

And this is where joy comes in. This is what makes the difference in our hearts, when the wrinkles on our faces are contours on topographical maps of well-lived lives. They represent the many journeys and pathways we have taken.

Joy comes from within us, just like the song's lyric: *"I've got that joy, joy, joy, joy down in my heart."* Joy offers us everlasting happiness. Joy is internal—down in our heart; happiness is external.

Do we always know the difference? Of course not, and discerning life's nuances is one of life's greatest challenges.

When my father got diagnosed with ALS, was he happy with the diagnosis? No, but he continued to radiate joy to his family and friends and coworkers. Was I happy? No, and I needed to catch up with his way of seeing things. I could not get past the possibility—which turned out to be the certainty—of losing my dad to something *so* horrible.

ALS is an unforgiving disease. It gradually robs the patient of their ability to walk, lift their arms, grasp things, scratch an itch, hug a loved one, speak, swallow, and breathe. There is hardly a happy thought in any of that reality. It's fatal.

Joy doesn't save us from horrific news, sadness, heartbreak, or even despair. Joy doesn't prevent us from getting hurt. Joy doesn't make us any less vulnerable.

For my father—and for me—joy meant believing in Jesus Christ and trying to radiate Him in *all* that we do. *Trying,* surely not always succeeding. And, of course, joy may mean something different to a practicing Buddhist, Muslim, or Hindu. But no matter how we measure, define, or experience it, joy is bigger than our external selves. It is bigger than our *current* happiness.

I shall not go so far as to define joy as our purpose. My dad didn't do that. He was never trying to be a philosopher or theologian, or offer riddles that could not be answered.

They say that money can't buy happiness. But it can. Money buys plenty of happiness. Vacations, cars, boats, power, second homes, pay-per-view, even sex. The age-old catch phrase should really be rebranded to "Money can't buy joy."

At our very core, we desire contentment in our lives. And maybe that is what joy offers us the most.

Living Life in the Beatitudes

"When he saw the crowds, he went up the mountain, and after he sat down, His disciples came to him." (Matthew 5:1) Jesus gave us the beautiful gift of the Beatitudes as a way of life that promises eternity in the Kingdom of God.

The Beatitudes are "blessing sayings," and they offer us a practical and simple life in discipleship. They are also comforters amid times of suffering, hurt, and testing. The Beatitudes are the lifeblood and beating heart of Christianity, a sacred lens with which to look at the world.

Jesus had been preaching throughout Galilee, and crowds were following Him. He had become a celebrity. He sees the multitudes looking for wisdom, so He goes up to the mountain and begins to speak to them. That's the setting.

I would like to briefly introduce you to a meditation practice called *Lectio Divina* (literally meaning *divine reading*). It's a traditional, monastic way of reading Scriptures. It's a way of becoming immersed and promoting communion with God through the living word by reading, reflecting, and responding to Scripture. Once you understand it, it's a way of learning and absorbing almost anything with practical application.

Close your eyes for a moment, take a deep breath, put the book or Kindle down on your lap. Sink into your chair or couch and take another deep breath. Nobody is watching; don't worry about it. You can pretend you fell asleep for a moment. Relax your shoulders, release the tension in your back, relax your legs, relax your feet—they're tired because you never stop running. There is always *so* much to do. Or as was sometimes the case at the peak of the pandemic, sometimes there was nothing to do, and nothing can be exhausting. Take another deep breath and relax your mind. If you can, take one minute, just sixty seconds, and do nothing, think of nothing. Be nothing. And once you've done that, come back, and let's very slowly read along together with an open heart and mind. It does not matter whether you read quietly to yourself or out loud. Consider trying it both ways.

> Blessed are the poor in spirit, for theirs is the kingdom of heaven.
>
> Blessed are those who mourn, for they will be comforted.
>
> Blessed are the meek, for they will inherit the earth.
>
> Blessed are those who hunger and thirst for righteousness, for they will be satisfied.
>
> Blessed are the merciful, for they will be shown mercy.
>
> Blessed are the pure in heart, for they will see God.

Blessed are the peacemakers, for they will be called children of God.

Blessed are they who are persecuted for the sake of righteousness, for theirs is the kingdom of heaven.

Blessed are you when people insult you and persecute you and utter every kind of evil against you falsely because of me. Rejoice and be glad, for your reward will be great in heaven.

After that first reading, do any words or phrases jump out to you? "Meek." What does that mean? "Merciful." Has someone hurt you or have you hurt someone for which you pray for forgiveness?

Anything catch your eye? Anything? What imagery stands out to you? "Persecution." What does that mean? Have you ever persecuted someone who is different from you? How do you feel about that? Have you ever been persecuted for who you are or what you believe? Is acceptance something you are looking for? Does anything else pop? And if nothing does, don't be concerned. There are no rules here.

Let's go through the reading again. Start by closing your eyes again, relaxing again, being open again, believing again. Listen. Read it slowly, maybe even more slowly than the first time. Be open to *receiving*. Consider a long pause after each verse. Ready?

Blessed are the poor in spirit, for theirs is the kingdom of heaven.

Blessed are those who mourn, for they will be comforted.

Blessed are the meek, for they will inherit the earth.

Blessed are those who hunger and thirst for righteousness, for they will be satisfied.

Blessed are the merciful, for they will be shown mercy.

Blessed are the pure in heart, for they will see God.

Blessed are the peacemakers, for they will be called children of God.

Blessed are they who are persecuted for the sake of righteousness, for theirs is the kingdom of heaven.

Blessed are you when people insult you and persecute you and utter every kind of evil against you falsely because of me. Rejoice and be glad, for your reward will be great in heaven.

Do you feel anything? Any nudge? Any pull? Is your heart speeding up or slowing down? Do you notice? Is God speaking to you in any way? Can you tell what He is saying? Are you smiling or does sadness overpower you? Listen more carefully.

Our final reading is even slower than the previous two. Continue to quiet your mind. Work can wait five more minutes, and so can the laundry. Empty everything. Everything. Slowly read the passage again.

Blessed are the poor in spirit, for theirs is the kingdom of heaven.

Blessed are those who mourn, for they will be comforted.

Blessed are the meek, for they will inherit the earth.

Blessed are those who hunger and thirst for righteousness, for they will be satisfied.

Blessed are the merciful, for they will be shown mercy.

Blessed are the pure in heart, for they will see God.

Blessed are the peacemakers, for they will be called children of God.

Blessed are they who are persecuted for the sake of righteousness, for theirs is the kingdom of heaven.

Blessed are you when people insult you and persecute you and utter every kind of evil against you falsely because of me. Rejoice and be glad, for your reward will be great in heaven.

What is it saying to you? Is there a dominant theme? Is there any one phrase that jumps off the page? Does anything call you to further prayer or contemplation? Are you called to action in some way?

"Hungry." What does it mean to be hungry? Are you hungry in any way? Are you hungry for food? What will the homeless person eat for dinner tonight? How can I help? Is there an invitation of some sort?

How does the reading challenge you? Let your imagination run wild.

I had never heard of *Lectio Devina* until I began studying for the diaconate. It's a beautiful, contemplative, and powerful learning tool for seekers. It's rich because it causes our hearts to slow and open like an oracle, and then it draws us to action.

The Beatitudes are timeless and filled with grace and opportunity. They are a ladder, a climb in many ways, an ascent of some sorts. They are a way for the excluded among us to feel included. The Beatitudes are about living a Christ-centered life. And yet, it does not matter what you believe or what religion you are. We can interpret them and apply them in *many* redemptive and valuable ways. We are all but people working hard to do our best every day. God understands that. He meets us where we are. In the end, it matters little what our background is. We all have a duty to take care of ourselves and each other, no matter what our belief system. And if we don't? We have *nothing*, nothing at all.

In the Beatitudes, Jesus teaches us about humility, charity, compassion, and love. We learn about grace and are inspired by the possibility of transformation in our lives and a *new* set of ideals for how we move from who we are to who we can become. That's a powerful challenge *regardless* of our religious beliefs. Let's face it, we all want to be the best version of ourselves, and the transformation process, realistically, is a lifelong journey.

My father lived his life in the Beatitudes, and when it came time to choose a Gospel reading for his funeral, it was the obvious selection. The Beatitudes were part of the Sermon on the Mount and offer instructions for the good life well-lived. They draw us in, moving us closer to the true self. For my dad, they offered a model of living and loving. That's the lesson. For a practical guy, they were simple and straight-forward, guiding principles of the servant leader, of the true disciple. Each Beatitude offers a *condition* and a *result*, making them workable, *possible*, efficient, and offering a future reward.

How do we respond to the Beatitudes in a very *practical* way? Let's break it down one by one.

Blessed are the poor in spirit, for theirs is the kingdom of heaven.

Be satisfied with what you have, no matter what it is, no matter how your wealth is measured. Practicing gratitude increases our appreciation for life. It's one of the alchemist's secrets. We've all seen plenty of people who have so much more and end up with nothing . . . not even a family. Not only was my father satisfied, he gave away his surplus. We're called to share what we have and to be generous to others.

Part of our life's work must be to care for those who don't get it, for those who frequently stumble and for those who *can't* take care of themselves—the refugee, the immigrant, the single mother, and those rejected by their families.

Starving for more? We often think of *poor* in material ways, as having few material things. But in a deeper sense, poor means having *nothing* at all. When we have nothing, when there is no other option, when we are overwhelmed by life, that's when we really can become close with God. Lean into Him. Once we real-ize we need God in our lives and that apart from Him we can do nothing, we surrender control rather than trying to handle everything on our own. And that surrender? It's the pathway to Heaven.

Blessed are those who mourn, for they will be comforted.

Grief and loss are overwhelming, and they're some of the toughest emotions that cause us to suffer. Reach out to those who are grieving; they need you *so* very much. The hug, the call, the text, the invitation to dinner, all matter.

My dad spent many of his nights checking in and comforting people who needed help or had suffered losses in their lives. My dad taught me how important such a simple gesture like that can be. If I have been so honored that you have asked me to preach the homily at the funeral for your loved one, I will be checking in with you and your family until the end of my days. There are so many who are too familiar with heavy tears and comforting others after they have experienced a loss is one of the most important things we can do.

Starving for more? God is the ultimate comforter. No matter what has happened in our lives, we can still be content because Christ wraps us in a warm blanket. And once we have found that contentment in our own lives, no matter what we mourn, once we have found sorrow in our own sins, that's when *we* can offer a quiet, warm blanket to others. When we enter the sacred space of another's grief, we truly mourn with them.

Blessed are the meek, for they will inherit the earth.

If I heard it once, I have heard it hundreds of times since my dad died—that people viewed him as unpretentious and humble. Humility is an interesting trait, in that it has some degree of paradox built into it. To have deep humility, one must first have a tremendous sense of self-worth. You have to know where you came from and what defines you.

In many ways, my dad submitted to God's will, the road to the true self. He wasn't one of those people who needed to hear himself speak. He possessed self-control. He didn't raise his voice to make a point.

The meek walk softly. They are satisfied no matter what their circumstances. The meek are like corner puzzle pieces, quiet but grounding. Get your ego out of the way and reflect on who you are underneath the hood. And when we find that person, that's when we are most in a position to become servant leaders. Humble hearts always enter the arena to help the unnoticed, the marginalized, and those who lack choice.

Starving for more? "Meek" is a word we have trouble getting our heads around. When Jesus speaks of the meek, He is referring to someone who is gentle, and someone who uses their passions in a just manner, most often for others. American journalist, social activist, and co-founder of the *Catholic Worker* newspaper, Dorothy Day, once wrote, "If we did works of mercy to be praised by men, or from pride and vanity and sense of power, then we had our reward. If we did them for the love of God, in whose image we have been made, then God would reward us; then we were doing them for a supernatural motive."

Blessed are those who hunger and thirst for righteousness, for they will be satisfied.

Many of the Beatitudes offer simple and complex learning opportunities. "Blessed are those who hunger" means that God is watching over those less fortunate, telling us of His preference for the poor.

Like my father, we are called to feed the hungry and clothe the naked. We are called to liberate the oppressed and those held in any type of bondage. On another level, "hunger" refers to our passion and desire and need for Christ in our lives. And whether we take the simple or complex view, maybe one follows the other. Those who hunger and thirst for righteousness stand up to the world's bullies on behalf of others. Many of society's hungriest are minimized, minimalized, and trivialized by the stronger and more powerful.

And so, should we really be sitting on the sidelines while someone *else* fixes things?

Starving for more? Hunger hurts. Thirst hurts. They can cause pain and discomfort. And when we feel pain, when we have a hole in our heart of any kind, Jesus fills it and makes it better. God meets us in our pain and reminds us, "I'm on your side." Isn't it satisfying to know we don't have to get to the top, that the blessing is often at the bottom of the mountain, in the middle of our own big mess?

Blessed are the merciful, for they will be shown mercy.

Showing mercy is about forgiveness, kindness, and compassion toward others. Are you quick to offer mercy or quick to place blame? Are you quick to work it out or quick to sue? Are you quick to forgive or do you carry a grudge? Do you look forward or are you always looking back?

We reap what we sow. I believe that. And yet, it *is* hard to show kindness to people who hurt us. I know this. At its best, hurt makes us resilient. At its worst, hurt causes a grudge, or even worse, a path of revenge.

My father died with no enemies. Unfortunately, at times, he got hurt in the crossfire of others, including crossfire from extended family squabbles. It hurt him. We had thought that my father's ALS journey was going to be a very tough road spanning many years, and yet he died less than a month after his diagnosis.

Those who demonstrate mercy *will* receive mercy.

Starving for more? Live by the Golden Rule: treat others as we wish to be treated. Sometimes we want to punish people for what they have done to us. But isn't it good to know that when we don't punish others for what they have done to us, we won't be punished for what we have not done in return? We are all sinners, and we all do bad things. Jesus calls us to, very simply, love each other as we wish to be loved.

Blessed are the pure in heart, for they will see God.

We have our outward selves and our inward selves. It's nice when they are the same. Is it even possible? "Let's make a deal," is an expression we've all heard countless times. That wasn't my father. He *never* did a favor or proffered his assistance seeking personal gain.

"What's in it for me?" We all know people who ask this question persistently. Sometimes God seems hidden from us. But Jesus tells us that the pure of heart shall see God and that inward holiness causes us to radiate Christ.

My father *glowed*. He glowed because He radiated God's goodness. We all know some people who seemingly work to create or aggravate conflict. The pure of heart tear down the walls of hatred and prejudice.

Starving for more? Sometimes we do things so that others have a positive view of us. It feels good when others see us in a good light. But Jesus is talking about doing the right things for the right reasons. When we not only change our actions, but our hearts, Christ is reminding us that we will see God. And as we offer that gift to others, out of pure love, we begin to see them as God sees them.

Blessed are the peacemakers, for they shall be called children of God.
Plain and simple: "Let there be peace on Earth, and let it begin with me." That's not complicated.

Like the song, peace starts with us. It *always* starts with us. It starts with reconciling *ourselves* with God.

How can peace start with us if we're initiating conflict? Peacemakers not only try to live peaceful and contemplative lives, but they also try to bring that peace and sense of calm to family, friends, neighbors, and coworkers.

Peace can change hearts. Through the years, my father was called on countless times to be the reconciler, the mediator, and the bridge. Isn't it beautiful when family members who have held onto hurts for decades are able to put them aside for all the right reasons?

Starving for more? The world is a complicated place—it has taught us to pick sides. What if we didn't? What if we chose not to go with the flow? What if we made our decisions based upon everyone winning, upon everyone flourishing, upon everyone finding peace and reconciliation in their lives? And when we make decisions in this way, when we imitate God's love for us, we become children of God.

Blessed are they who are persecuted for the sake of righteousness, for theirs is the kingdom of heaven.

Have you ever been treated badly for what you believed? Have people gossiped about you? Has the conversation ever stopped when you walked into the room?

Have you ever been excluded by the in-crowd or the work clique? What's happened to *you* when you have stood up *to* others or *for* others?

Sometimes what we believe will fall on the side of the majority. At other times, it will fall on the side of the minority, and that's when our voice is called to be firmest and loudest. My father had a certain *Atticus Finch* quality to him, the character from Harper Lee's *To Kill a Mockingbird*. Like Atticus, my father stood for fairness, equality, and moral uprightness. He sometimes found himself in the minority on numerous social issues—and was persecuted for it— including important zoning and abutter matters when he was promoting affordable housing for families and the elderly.

Starving for more? When Jesus faced persecution, so did His followers. If I speak out, am I willing to suffer for it? It happens more often than not. Am I daring enough to be that voice? And those who do? They will receive the kingdom of Heaven. And if we are never persecuted for following Christ, maybe we should ask how big our voice is and how visibly we are living for Him.

Blessed are you when people insult you and persecute you and utter every kind of evil against you falsely because of me. Rejoice and be glad, for your reward will be great in heaven.

Ever been the Democrat on vacation with a bunch of Republicans? Ever been the Republican at a dinner table filled with a bunch of Democrats? Never did we see the extremes of perspective as we did with the 2020 presidential election, and the 2022 midterms.

Tax breaks for the rich, social service programs for the poor. We all have a different way of looking at the right way to solve "it," no matter what "it" is.

It's the same with religion. No matter what we believe, do we shout it from the rooftops regardless of the consequences? Or do we politely nod our heads and avoid the controversy?

Do we deny, or do we evangelize what we believe? My father believed in the Creed of the Catholic Church and was always happy to discuss, debate, and defend it. And if you had a different type of belief system, he was open to listening, was intrigued by the differences, and applauded your enthusiasm for believing in something bigger than yourself.

Starving for more? This Beatitude is like the previous one, in that it references being persecuted for Jesus. You can still be happy when people hurt you, or when they say mean things, because as we have learned from many other heroes in the Bible, the reward will be great.

When we live a life in the Beatitudes, that's when we get a glimpse into the heart of God, and it's the most beautiful thing imaginable. It's as close as we get to Heaven on Earth because we know that God is on our side. My father radiated Christ, and that was the indescribable quality that made him shine.

Blessed means happy, and isn't there an *enormous* difference between happy and unhappy people? My dad was happy through his generosity, in his concern for others, in the way he took care of those who need us most . . . in his empathy for what was going on in the lives of so many, in his ability to engage for the better good.

Living life in the Beatitudes isn't easy. And yet, they help to reveal what's written on our hearts. If we want the kingdom of Heaven, are we prepared to lose everything else? The Beatitudes represent Jesus pulling back the curtain on the mystery of His kingdom. Living life in the Beatitudes requires a foundational change in how we live our lives and our obligations to each other, but the promise of making that change is salvation.

Savoring

Before I so much as opened my laptop for the first time, I had these chapters outlined in my head.

I had never set out to write a book. I was far too busy with family, work, church, and volunteer activities . . . and, of course, I was quite busy with my grief, which had become a constant companion, and held my attention for a good part of my days. It still does, only in a subtler way.

I started by, simply and practically, writing down memories about my dad. I did not want to forget him, and I did not want my kids to forget him, as that would be the biggest sin of all. Besides the frequent visits to the cemetery, besides sometimes sitting at his dark walnut desk at work for inspiration on important topics, writing had become an outlet. Individual memories turned into larger themes, and those themes, when packaged, became chapters, without my even knowing it.

A book had been planted, watered with tears, and sunned with smiles.

Along the way, I realized I did have time, especially for something so important. The kids were in school and working, and the pandemic had stolen many of my church and volunteer activities. And, like so many other companies, my office had gone remote, saving an endless number of commuting hours and travel back and forth to clients. Yes, I had time . . . and you do, too. We all have a journey, so write down yours. It's important that you do it, for your family.

In those larger themes, I never considered writing about leisure activities. They were simple *pursuits*, not grandiose topics like life and death, and good and evil. Where were the lessons? And yet, though these things may not be *objectively* important, they were very important to me and my family. They still are. I do not think I had realized the impact of our family leisure time until I sifted through the many family photos and albums which recounted an endless array of activities and memorable, family gatherings. All of them were precious, though maybe, sadly, I did not realize how precious until much later.

"15-2, 15-4, 15-6, and a pair for eight," my father said confidently.

"I have a double run and the right jack," my son Brian brightly responded. "It's my kitty, too."

In case you are not familiar, those are cribbage terms; cribbage has been a staple at our house for decades. Brian is a cribbage devotee—voted most likely to have a cribbage board in his backpack—*and* an extra deck of cards. Unlike chess, which requires no player dialogue, cribbage relies on pegging, and the spoken word of counting out your hand for your opponent. Ask any of my kids how they learned how to play cribbage, and they will tell you with a wide smile and without hesitation, "Papa," their endearing name for my dad.

Cribbage is a classic card game originating in the 1600s. It's played with a standard deck of cards, small pegs, and a "scoring track," appropriately called a cribbage board. We likely have dozens of cribbage boards in the family—big and small, wooden and metal, simple and elaborate, rectangular and circular, cheap, and far too expensive. They are in drawers, on countertops, and in my kids' drawstring beach bags. I have a small, oval, faux-ivory board that I bought in Nantucket with Lisa many years ago . . . it's still one of my favorites. Then there is the "29" board, representing the perfect cribbage hand . . . a Jack and three fives, and the "cut card" which is a five in the same suit as the Jack. The odds of getting the perfect hand are only one in 216,580, making it easier to get diagnosed with ALS than it is to unearth the perfect cribbage hand. And, of course, there is the large mahogany board with beautiful, metal pegs given to me by Lisa's beloved grandmother, Nana.

The year after my dad died, my best friend, John, and his husband, Colin, gave Lisa and me a light oak, square wooden board with a map of Cape Cod burned into the middle. The oldest board at my mom and dad's house is likely a simple, homemade, Navy ship owned by my Uncle Frank, passed to his daughter, Ann, who is my cousin and godmother on my mom's side, and later given to my father by her.

And the most precious boards? Probably the cheapest ones, the ones that sometimes get lost or misplaced, perhaps bought at the airport on our way on a family vacation, or the ones from the *honkytonk* gift shop en route to *somewhere* because they were signs of good things to come.

One of the photos that forever lives in the attic of my brain is a collage of the same photo of my dad on different family vacations wearing one of his long-sleeved t-shirts and a fishing-type hat to keep the sun from beating on his blotchy head—the too-frequent site of previous skin cancers—while playing cribbage with my boys by a hotel or cruise ship pool, all of them with shirts off and likely sunburned. If you were studying the photos, you were not quite sure whether they were advertisements for Bud Light, Ray-Ban, or Quicksilver boardshorts. And they did not just play; the lesson was only partly about game strategy. They talked about school, dating, summer jobs, politics, the stock market, draft picks, and the upcoming sports season—whatever it may have been. In many ways, maybe without even realizing it, they talked about the good life well-lived. And though cribbage—and often the game of spoons—were a mainstay of Martin family travel, some of the best games occurred at our kitchen table, the coffee table in the parlor, or on the back porch.

Consider learning how to *play* cribbage and giving cribbage boards as gifts. What's fun about giving them as a gift is that if the recipient does not know how to play, you have an obligation to teach them, and the pedagogy usually takes hours upon hours of good conversation, potato chips and pretzels, and a Diet Coke or gin & tonic. Many lasting friendships can be made over a great white shark or baseball diamond–shaped cribbage board.

My dad was practical, but he *savored* life. He savored family, food, summer, and those simple pastimes like cribbage.

Savoring is an art. How often do we rush from one thing to the next? How many times do we gobble down our supper to get the dishes done so we can catch our favorite reality show at 8:00? We sit down to enjoy a good book, but do we have any idea what we just read in those last ten to fifteen pages?

"Savoring" sounds like it should involve a picnic blanket and croissant in Paris, pushing the grandchildren in a stroller in Disney World, or singing and swaying around the piano on Christmas Eve. And those are beautiful, pastel moments to savor for sure. But mostly, savoring is about slowing down and relishing the present moment and knowing you are alive. It's about finding joy in life's simplest pleasures.

My dad enjoyed engaging in the lost art of conversation, talking slowly—never rushing—and always with purpose. He ate his steak and buttered baked potato one enjoyable bite at a time, as he did his hot dogs and beans and grilled cheese and tomato. He read every word with expression. He acted out every charade in form and character. He danced and sang with purpose. He never played the game to win. He played the game to have the richest experience possible, with whomever he had the pleasure of being with at the time.

And to be in the present moment, to be able to savor, my dad did not multitask, he did one thing at a time. When we do too much, we remember none of it, and we do none of it well. Unlike me, my dad did not worry, and did not spend too much time in the past *or* in the future. He planned, of course, but, on those simpler things, he did not wander too far from the present. Why would he?

How often do we take the time to feel how cold the snow is before we shovel it away? Do we catch the aroma of the fresh, baked bread coming out of the oven at the local bakery? Can we hear what the other person is saying, or are we just waiting for the right moment for them to catch their breath so we can interrupt and say that which is far more important? Savoring involves *all* our senses.

Lisa has often played impromptu wedding planner. She did it at the wedding rehearsal of a couple whose marriage I was to celebrate a day or two later. And despite all the energy of the bridal party, and having to calm anxious parents who wanted everything to be just perfect, as the bride stood at the back of the church, about to process down the long aisle, Lisa whispered in the bride's ear, as she always does, "Just take it all in and the walk will take a lifetime. See who's in the aisle, smell the flowers, remember the smiles, be mindful of your breath and the beating of your heart, notice how the sun is coming through the church windows, look for the little kids hanging off the pews, and walk slowly . . . be in the present moment . . . cherish it . . . and you'll remember it forever."

When we find joy in the present moment and *truly* savor it, it slows life down, and it allows us to linger and loiter and be idle for a bit longer. And though it requires practice, intention, and gratitude, it *is* a way of cheating time. Just a little. And isn't that something we are all looking for?

Our Sunday routine is pretty much the same every week. Sure, it's changed with the kids in college, and it's changed some more with the isolation of the pandemic. As a deacon, I often assist at two Sunday masses, perhaps preaching at one or both. After church, Lisa and I sometimes go for a long hike in the Blue Hills Reservation just minutes from our house, seven thousand acres of hiking trails with gorgeous views of downtown Boston. And then? The food and games begin.

For some families, Sunday means a leisurely, hot cup of coffee and the *New York Times*. Sounds perfect—but that was not *our* Sunday, especially in autumn. Fall Sundays brought football, and everyone wore their Patriots team jerseys, gifts from Lisa and me. We all wore them . . . the kids, my parents, and Lisa's parents. And if you were a Martin family boyfriend or girlfriend, you got a jersey, too. On Sunday, we play second string.

Come as a guest before the game and the menu includes some assortment of cheese and crackers, kielbasa, buffalo chicken dip, nachos with all of the fixings, shrimp cocktail, artichoke dip with toasted pita, and chips 'n dip. And at halftime? No matter the weather, something is usually on the grill . . . burgers and dogs, steak tips, roast beef sliders, or BBQ ribs. And potatoes, always some kind of potatoes—baked, mashed, scalloped, or steak fries. And if not the grill, something is in the crockpot, like homemade chili, pulled pork, Swedish meatballs, Italian wedding soup, or beef stew. If time was short because the hike went long, or too many babies had to be baptized that day . . . maybe it was a cold cut platter of baked ham, provolone, rare roast beef, mortadella, prosciutto, Genoa salami, capicola and footlong, crusty baguettes . . . and potato salad.

We have a large family room overlooking the back porch and deep woods in the back of the house. In the dew of morning, it is not uncommon to see deer, wild turkeys, or a coyote. The room has a stone fireplace, player piano, couches, and comfy chairs and coffee tables that usually have dozens of stacked books and an unfinished puzzle at least fully framed. But the most important piece of furniture is a chess table, an actual wooden table that looks like a card table, one of my favorite finds from Ethan Allen.

"You gave up your queen too early in the game," my dad said to Meghan.

"I have a plan," Meghan responded wryly. It was quite possible that there was a plan, or maybe not, but she was deliberate in her words and actions, often wearing a Mona Lisa smile. But what was even more deliberate? From every family vacation, there is a precious photo of my dad and Meghan from behind, sharing a quiet moment, walking hand-in-hand along the touristy streets of a foreign country. They delighted in one another's company.

Chess is also part of the Sunday routine. Ask any of my kids how they learned how to play chess, and they will tell you with a wide smile, "Papa." Tournaments last for hours. And the winner may take on a new challenger, or two new players may move into the high-back, leather chairs.

It is sometimes said that the student becomes the master in his or her ability, and that is probably what happened with my son Kevin. Kevin is a fierce competitor and was captain of his high school chess team at St. Sebastian in Needham, the high school that two of my father's brothers attended. Kevin was also co-captain of the Seb's sailing team. There is nothing quite like watching your son sail on the Charles River with the Boston skyline reflecting peacefully on the still water.

If you asked Kevin what sailing was all about, he would politely tell you, "Chess on water." My dad still won his share of games against all the kids, but win or lose, he savored every one of them.

And then there was golf. Ask any of my kids how they learned how to play golf, and they will tell you with a wide smile, "Papa." My dad was their first golf instructor, and a patient one at that.

"Wow, Connor, nice shot," my father said. "You might put that on in two," he added.

"I know, Papa, but like you say, you drive for show and putt for dough," Connor responded. Connor listened well and picked up many of my dad's expressions and street colloquialisms. Over the years, Connor's driver shot became longer and my dad's shorter. But after a good walk in the woods retrieving lost balls, and the final thud, they still battled it out on the green.

I have golfed some of the country's greatest courses with my dad, and a few in Ireland as well. He took up the game late, probably in his forties. From Pebble Beach to the Links at Spanish Bay, from Harbour Town in Hilton Head to the Seaside Course at Sea Island, there are many memories and many more lessons: humility, maturity, patience, perspective, the importance of practice, trust, comfort in silence, and understanding that pressure is part of the game, and that the most important shot is not the last one, but the next one.

Golf has a way of shaping not only the player but people. My dad had two home clubs: Granite Links in Quincy, with sweeping views of Boston, and Ocean Edge on Cape Cod. I stopped playing golf about fifteen years ago; two herniated discs at C5 and C6 will sometimes do that. Next-day pain was just not worth it anymore. If golf taught me anything, it taught me that not everything goes as it should.

When my father died, we went back to Granite Links where my dad's golf clubs graced the entrance to the buffet. The clubs are now at my mom's house in the attic. She is reluctant to separate them, but I think we have concluded that when the kids need a replacement club, they can take it from Papa's bag; that way everyone gets something along the way when they need it.

Every avid golfer has his or her share of bad golf jokes. My dad was no different, and he told many with a contagious sense of humor. This was one of his favorites, and I remember him retelling it for the hundredth time just weeks before he died.

> This guy Shamus, you know, was an avid golfer and was teeing up for a very tough shot. At the exact moment, a long funeral procession went by. Shamus stopped, took off his scally, put it over his heart, and bowed his head.
>
> One of his three golfing buddies looked at him and said, "Shamus, that was very kind and mighty decent of you. I'm really quite touched."
>
> Shamus responded, "Yeah, I know. It's the least I could do. We would have been married thirty-four years on Tuesday."

The summer before my dad died, he put both of his golf memberships on hold. It was very hard for him, but my sense is that he thought it was temporary and that he would be back to it the next year. He knew he had health issues going on, but just didn't know what they were when it was time for his membership renewal. But in that last summer, the kids still took him out in the cart when they played. And he still offered pointers, charging them with good etiquette, and they talked about everything and anything.

As I look back at that last summer, there was so much to be thankful for. My dad and I attended some early season Red Sox games at Fenway Park, and sat in the same third-base seats we had been sitting in for over twenty-five years. Meghan graduated from high school, and Connor graduated from college in North Carolina. My and Lisa's parents made the trip with us. We took a family Baltics and Scandinavian cruise, and it was as if time stood still. We even played cribbage on our stateroom deck in Russia and biked around Copenhagen (my dad not participating in the latter, naturally). We dropped Meghan off at Penn State in August and stayed an extra night in the Poconos, and my dad so enjoyed the ride and interacting with the kids.

The Penn State University Park campus is enormous, and my dad was, mostly, in a wheelchair at that point. I do not have one photo of him in the wheelchair; it is a memory I've chosen to suppress, with no record of it. We played Pictionary over Labor Day weekend on Cape Cod. And of the last two photos I have of my dad, one is of him and my mom, walking back to our Cape house on the front walkway, holding hands of course, Mom carrying a small bag of M&Ms they would share after dinner. The other is one of me and my dad playing checkers in rocking chairs on a beer barrel checkers board on the front porch of a nearby restaurant.

He died a week later, but got so much out of that last summer, and we savored *every* bit of it.

Dark Turns into Light

Drive-in theaters, Elvis, going steady, *Father Knows Best, The Ed Sullivan Show.*

I should have grown up in the fifties and sixties. They were happy days and simpler times. And I love the music from that era. Nowadays, it's not too often that you can dance to "The Twist," "The Stroll," or "The Tennessee Waltz"—unless it's your second cousin's second wedding.

One of my favorite songs has always been "Stand by Me," originally performed in 1961 and written by singer-songwriter Ben E. King. Do you know the words? Can you feel the tenderness? Does it invoke a memory? Close your eyes and sway to it. The song has that familiar doowop sound and invokes many strong feelings. It's a melody about love but not *any* kind of love. It's about *enduring* love, a love that survives the ups and downs, a love that survives the most difficult days, a love that stands the test of time.

What I didn't know—and likely *should* have—is that verse two is a Bible verse, specifically Psalm 46:3. "Thus we do not fear, though earth be shaken and mountains quake to the depths of the sea."

The Psalm encourages us to hope and trust in God and in His grace. It beckons us to *not* be afraid and to find joy *even* on the most sorrowful of days.

My dark night began in the spring of 2019. Like heart disease, it didn't happen overnight. I could start to feel cracks in my spiritual footing. We walked into every one of my father's doctor's appointments filled with hope and possibility and encouragement, only to have the rug pulled out from underneath us at every turn. When the healing ministers said "yes," the doctors said "no."

My optics were changing. I had always looked at life through rose-colored glasses, and my spectacles had shattered.

When I first began to pray about the possibility of being ordained a deacon, I couldn't turn God off. He was driving me nuts. He was like a loud radio in my ear. I heard Him at work, on the crowded soccer field, at the movies, and while working out at the gym. He was becoming a considerable distraction to my everyday life. God a distraction? Usually, we think of our life distracting us from our desire for God. At this moment, God was distracting me from the desire for my life. He was pushing me *too* much to engage. And then I gave in. I said yes. And once I did, I could control the volume of the God radio.

That's the relationship God and I had for a very long time. He tugged, I leaned in. He pulled, I leaned in. But one day, sometime along the road of my dad's illness—or so it seemed—He was gone, almost as if someone unplugged the radio that had become so important to me. I felt abandoned by God. Forsaken. Empty. Alone. Angry. Sad. Anxious. Dejected.

"God, where are you?"

"God, we could really use a little help here."

"God, seriously, are you paying attention or what?"

"God, your faithful servant is dying, please get in the ring with us?"

"God, are you listening at all right now?"

"God, do you hear the cries coming from this family?"

You pay into the insurance policy for fifty or sixty years, only to find out there is no coverage when you need it most? It didn't seem fair.

I had never had a faith crisis before, and over time, I came to realize that I was smack dab in the middle of one. My heart was skipping a beat for all the *wrong* reasons. I was in a dark night of the soul. I was the one that people came to for answers, and—suddenly—I mostly had questions. I was questioning things I had always accepted as truth. Things that I thought were always black and white now felt gray to me. Not everything, but many, many things.

The water was rising around me. I was suffocating and could not catch my breath. I first thought I was just in a funk.

After some soul-searching, I came to realize it was *much* more than that.

―――――――――

The first writings about the dark night of the soul came from St. John of the Cross, a sixteenth-century Spanish mystic and Carmelite monk. He wrote an eight-stanza poem entitled "Dark Night of the Soul," which recounted his spiritual darkness. It was an incredibly painful time for him. And yet he talked about how the time was transformational and how that transformation offered promise and hope. He spoke of how the soul moves from distractions and life's entanglements and difficulties to a place of peace, harmony, and contentment.

According to St. John, the dark night is synonymous with finding the "narrow way" about which Jesus spoke. (Matthew 7:13-14) When you think of *some way*, you think about some type of progress being made. And when we think of the *narrow way*, or the narrow gate, we think about taking those progressive steps toward Christ. He is the way. He is the truth. He is the life. Walking His way means to walk as He walked. We follow in His footsteps, living as He lived.

The gate was *too* narrow for me. For me, the dark night meant a period in which hope seemed to be lost. External things like my dad's diagnosis with ALS, and his death, came out of nowhere and interfered with what I thought was the joy in my life.

I was having physical symptoms in my dark night . . . headaches, muscle twitching, tingling sensations, intense dreams, muscles cramps, and insomnia. Lisa was as supportive as she could be, but I felt isolated and stuck. I was even fearful to preach at church because I didn't want to deliver a debauched Gospel message. In the hospital, when the writing was on the wall, my dad knew that my mom and I were not buying into the prognosis, and it was my dad who *continued* to guide us. In one of his journal notes, he wrote, "Claire, believe them—have faith in God and them." *Them* meant the MGH doctors.

Mother Theresa was said to have had a dark night of the soul that lasted for the last fifty years of her life. She did not feel the presence of God, and yet she continued to radiate Him. I couldn't hear Him, and I couldn't feel Him.

And somehow, over time, light was shining in the dark corners. I came to realize that I was stuck, and there is a difference between being stuck and *not* knowing it and being stuck and knowing it. Along the way, grace kicked in. It was there all along. Like in *Evan Almighty*, does God offer us grace on a platter, or does he give us situations to find the grace? I had been confident that I had already found my true self, but this yearlong stretch caused me to realize that I was nowhere near where I thought I was on my journey. And, yet, without realizing it, I was continuing to grow. "No pain, no gain." I was surrendering to God *again*. I concluded that unknowingly *I* had kicked the plug out of the God radio, and it was God who plugged it back in.

Death tears at our faith. A parent dying is a rite of passage. I slowly started to accept that truth. A parent is going to die from something . . . a heart attack, cancer, and sure, maybe, ALS.

I had come to recognize, again, the full life with which I was blessed. Family lifted me up. Friends lifted me up. Work colleagues lifted me up. Parishioners lifted me up. One of my biggest fears of being an only child was not having brothers and sisters to lean on when one of my parents died. I quickly realized that I had dozens of brothers and sisters, who swooped in and put a net under me. *So* many people lifted me up.

My purpose started to return. A smile started to return. I was reminded that suffering is part of life. I sharpened my empathy skills.

I am drawn to others who are hurting or who have lost loved ones. I'm an empath by nature, keenly aware of others and what they need emotionally.

In the final year of my diaconate program, I had to write a paper on my charism, or at least what I perceived it to be. A charism is a gift from God, a gift of grace for the service of others. The assignment required prayer and contemplation.

In religious terms, a charism is grace bestowed on us. And it was important to reflect on this, because our charism is the lens through which we preach and minister. My charism is gratitude. I look at life through the lens of appreciation, and once I regained my footing, I called on that charism to help me through the narrow gate.

I miss my dad terribly. Sometimes I burst into tears for no apparent reason. A song. Seeing golfers ride by the patio of our summer house. His empty office. The missing chair on holidays. His laugh. His good input on some matter. But somehow, like the flower that emerges from the concrete, light emerged from the dark. Experiencing suffering is to walk with Christ, and we use that dark night as a catalyst for our own growth. If we are going to go through it, why not come out stronger?

In the end, love decided everything. Prayer, meditation, contemplation, hot yoga, having family and friends who were willing to listen—it helped. Staying close to church—it helped. Not rushing back to my prior life—it helped. Embracing the dark night once I realized I was in it—it not only helped, but I also feel like it brought forth a powerful breakthrough in my faith and growth as a human being. Believing, truly believing—it helped.

> *No, I won't be afraid*
> *Oh, I won't be afraid*
> *Just as long as you stand, stand by me.*

And He did.

Signs

Out of nowhere, my chest grew tight and my heart began to race. Faster and faster and faster.

I took a couple of aspirin.

I didn't think it could beat so fast. It felt as if my insides were about to explode. "I need to get to the hospital, I think I'm having a heart attack," I shouted to Lisa and my father. I took another aspirin, maybe three.

March 16, 2007. We were on our last night of school vacation week in Hilton Head. It was a week of beach, golf, family fun, and food. That was pre–herniated disc golf. I felt sweaty and had an impending sense of doom. *I should take two more aspirin,* I said to myself.

After five miles in the car and four more aspirin, we made it to the ER. I collapsed in the hospital lobby. A quick EKG indicated no heart attack. And yet, my heart rate was up to 320 bpm and climbing.

"Mr. Martin, I think you have an electrical condition known as supraventricular tachycardia, or SVT," the doctor calmly explained to me. "At this point, the only practical way to get your heart to slow down to a normal beat is to stop it completely through an IV push of a drug called Adenosine."

"OK, let's just do that, then," I said.

"Now, in the remote chance your heart doesn't click over on its own, my team will use a defibrillator to help your body get it going."

"What's that mean? Like those paddles? Walk me through..."

"Let's get this moving right now."

"Just do it, my heart's about to explode!" I shouted. I felt a gravity weighing my body down.

"Mr. Martin, calm down. We need you to calm down," the doctor instructed me.

"Seriously?"

"Mr. Martin, I want you to focus on that little, square, white calendar on the wall. See it? We're going to have your wife and father wait outside."

"OK," I said as tears rolled down my cheeks.

I fixated on that little, square, white calendar on the wall that had nothing on it but the date, "3/16," and, in very small letters, the name of a local ambulance company.

A nurse smiled at me, held my hand, and said, "You're going to be OK, just calm down."

Pushhh. Pushhh. Pushhh. I saw something fill the IV in my arm. And my heart stopped.

It didn't slow down. It stopped.

I couldn't hear it. I couldn't feel it. I couldn't sense it. I felt the breath go out of me. Stay with me, take a deep breath, and hold it.

One . . . two . . . three. Black and white postcards from my childhood slowly flashed before my eyes.

Four . . . five. I did as I was told and stayed focused on that little, square, white calendar. The nurse squeezed my hand tighter. "You're doing great," I remember her saying.

Six. I felt everything become hazy, cloudy, and blurred.

Where did my heart go? I thought to myself.

Seven . . . eight. The little, square, white calendar on the wall got bigger and bigger. The postcards of my life were advancing faster and faster through the years, faster than a deck of cards running through an automatic card shuffler. Faster and faster and faster.

Nine . . . ten. It seemed like forever.

Eleven seconds later, my heart started beating again. I could hear it. I could feel it. Exhale.

I felt the breath come into me. A tremendous warmth came over my body, like an electric blanket had been plugged in and put over me.

I was alive. This much I knew.

Some weeks later, I was on Cape Cod at a client meeting, and when I was leaving, as I would always do, I stopped at the local bookstore in Hyannis. As I pulled up to the store, every window—*every* window—was dressed in a large, square, white poster for a newly released book entitled *3:16: The Numbers of Hope* by Max Lucado.

Looking at those window treatments reminded me so much of that little, square, white calendar that I had stared at so intently in the hospital that evening. "For God so loved the world, that He gave His only Son, so that everyone who believes in Him will not perish, but have eternal life." (John 3:16)

Boom! It was a sign.

It was *more* than a sign. It was a conversion experience.

I didn't realize it at the time. God had been talking to me that night in the hospital. I had been on the fence about Him for a while, a reluctant disciple in many ways. I had not been listening to the other signs, the gentle tugs at my heart along the way. The word of God had been planted in my soul and my life was changed forever. Within a year, I would apply to the diaconate program, and five years later I would be ordained. I would become a preacher. Along the way, I would complete a Master of Arts in Ministry.

To this day, 3:16 follows me everywhere—everywhere—through seeming coincidences, including, most recently, the birthday of my editor, Rob.

We have two extra-large candles on our front porch sitting in big, bronze Pottery Barn candle holders. You know the ones, right? Don't worry, we bought them on sale. The candles are battery-operated but hadn't worked for years . . . maybe for as much as a decade. I used to put them on for parties, Christmas Eve and other special occasions, "a sign of hospitality, to set the welcoming mood." Over time, too many batteries, too many screws, too much rain, too much rust—it just wasn't worth it. They looked fine from a distance, au naturale.

About a month after my dad died, I noticed that one of the candles was on . . . and later it was off. A few days later, it happened again. And again.

A couple of Fridays later, Lisa and I were driving down the driveway, coming home from dinner and a movie, talking about my dad, and the candle was on again, apparently welcoming us home. Lisa and I looked at each other and grinned.

"What's that about?" I remember Lisa saying.

"I decided it's my dad saying hi," I responded.

"Maybe it is."

"I was joking."

"I know. I wasn't."

"Seriously?"

"Could be."

"Let's keep an eye on it." I decided to be practical and watch the data, just like my dad would do.

The candle remained dark, until a few days later, and then it came on again. What first caught my eye became intermittent and, within weeks, became the norm. It didn't go on at the same time every night; that was the most unpredictable part of it. It was hardly on a timer. The candle might make its presence known after dinner, but more often than not, after eight o'clock, and always before I went to bed around midnight.

The candle had become part of our lives. It was always there for us. It welcomed us home late at night. It guided us when taking out the trash. It caused us to laugh and to cry and to recall stories of my dad. It caused me to keep checking on it. It had become part of the nightly routine of shutting down the house.

As I went to bed at night, and rounded the staircase at the landing, the candle was always on and, no matter how tired I was, I stopped, paused, smiled, and said goodnight to my father. And, in response, the candle flickered back as if to offer a tender grin, at the pace of a warm and steady heartbeat.

It had been an emotional week. Aside from this chapter, I finished a rough draft of *All Is Well* on March 10, 2019, exactly six months after my dad's death. I didn't plan it that way.

It was a sad time, and I had recently started a nine-day novena to St. Patrick. It was during his captivity that St. Patrick's spirituality deepened because, in his hardships, he turned to prayer. I could relate.

March 17, 2020. It was St. Patrick's Day, barely. Oh, the drums go bang and the cymbals clang, and the horns they blaze away. The coronavirus had seemingly taken hold of us. The nation was shutting down, it just didn't know it yet. Boston barricaded its doors and was closed for business. Bars and restaurants were cancelled, and our beloved parade was, too. We stayed up late that night watching *The Quiet Man*, with John Wayne and Maureen O'Hara, known for its lush photography of the Irish countryside and a great, comedic, fistfight scene.

We bumped into Maureen O'Hara in Killarney, Ireland in the nineties. I wish I knew then that she and my mom shared the same birthday.

When the movie ended, we performed the nightly ritual of making sure that the doors were locked, put Zack and Chloe, our miniature labradoodles, to bed, turned off the kitchen lights, and walked up the stairs to our bedroom.

The candle was off. What? It didn't make any sense.

My book had been finished a week earlier. The novena was complete. The last day the candle lit the way for us was March 16 . . . 3:16.

It was six months to the day of my dad's funeral.

Another sign? Did my dad stay by my side for six months to make sure I was alright? Did he come to us through the light, the energy of the candle, an electrical disturbance, or through the number 316? I don't know, but it brings a smile to my face to think about it.

I, ultimately, needed a procedure to fix the electrical short circuit in my heart that had been correctly diagnosed in Hilton Head. All is well on the heart front, now many triathlons later.

And, by the way, if you ever think you are having a heart attack, you only need to take one aspirin. A dozen doesn't work twelve times better.

The Excerpts

In the 2003 drama, *Big Fish*, Edward Bloom, played by Albert Finney, becomes ill. His son, William, played by Billy Crudup, travels to be with him.

They have a difficult relationship. Will always believed that Edward told too many tall tales about his life, and never really told the truth.

In the final scene, Will takes his father to the river to set him free, giving Edward an opportunity to say goodbye to all the people in his life. Will sees the people who were the basis for Edward's grand embellishments, and at the funeral William comes to understand his father's life. It's a very emotional scene, and although it is sad, it's a celebration.

As much as you can't fathom or believe it, one day *you will die*.

Close your eyes for a moment. Take a deep breath. Take one more deep breath. Smell the incense. Don't worry about not having shoes, you don't need them. Hear the music. Maybe the deep breath doesn't so much matter.

You died. You died six days ago. The funeral parlor did a good job. Just enough makeup, not too much. It looks natural. They've gathered today for *you*. Stretch out a bit. The pallbearers have slowly rolled you down the church's center aisle.

I know. It's a weird thought. But relax and take refuge for a moment. Everything is beautiful, in its own way. There are many tears. All are sad at your unexpected departure. The church has quite a few people in it; maybe it would have been more, had it been Saturday.

You are in no pain. None. Later, maybe over beers, many will tell stories of your life, and what will they say?

Right now, standing at the pulpit before you, the preacher has eight to twelve minutes to capture you. And so, he or she starts, "Joe was a fine man. He was a good husband, a loving father, and a loyal member of the club for years."

Or how about, "Judy was a wonderful mother. All of the neighbors loved her cheery smile and willingness to help."

That took eight seconds. How will the preacher use the rest of his or her time? What will be said? How will your life be summarized?

My father wrote his own homily through his faith, his love of family, and his good works. He made it easy for me to speak his truth. Even in death, he continues to teach me and inspire me. My mom and I received over seven hundred cards, notes, emails, and texts about my dad. I wanted to share a few excerpts with you.

"He was so very kind and caring and engaging."

"Everyone respected him so much for the person that he was."

"I always enjoyed hearing the stories he told."

"Kevin was the most patient person I have ever met. He always took the time to ask about my kids and how my day was going."

"Your dad was awesome. That's all I can say."

"We will miss him dearly. He always had a smile on his face. He always did more than what was asked of him. I always looked forward to seeing a call come in from him."

"Every time he helped us, he did it anonymously. He didn't ask for any recognition. He was always working to make the world a little bit better."

"He took me to my very first Red Sox game and I will never forget it."

"Your father was a very holy man."

"Kevin taught me that ANY calculation CAN be done without pen and paper. You just need to be a genius like him to do it!"

"Your dad's love of family and community were always the first things he talked about as we started our annual planning meeting. He was so proud of you and I was always inspired by him."

"Your dad was a special guy—good humored, charismatic, sharp and wise. He was an extraordinary man, a positive force and touched the hearts of so many."

"I sat next to a woman at the funeral that I didn't know. She told me about a lot of great times with your family. She told me about how your father helped to save the church we were in and how the entire community will always remember him for that."

"Your father was a very nice person and was always very kind to me. I would not be in business had it not been for him.

He made it easy for me to sleep at night. I remember the first time he came to my office, he commented on the plaques I had on my wall for supporting some of the local sports and things. And then I came to your office, and I see pictures of him with US presidents. I was very humbled. He never talked to me like a customer, he talked to me like a friend. I always appreciated that about him."

"Look at you. Look at what you've done with your life. Now look at your father. What did you expect? He was such a role model. His kindness and commitment to service got passed down through you."

"He was a saint."

"You don't know me but I read your father's obituary in *The Globe* and I was very touched by his life. I got your email from your company website. Your father's life spoke to me. He left a legacy of love, leadership and giving back. His story inspired me to do a little more. No need to respond to me, just know that I, like many readers today, will find his life story a great example of a life well lived."

"What an enormous loss for all of us. I was always so impressed with his loyalty, kindness and generosity not only to his extended family but to the entire community, all in his quiet and humble way."

"Your dad taught me so much professionally and personally. He led by example, he instilled values of giving back, and that life is about more than yourself and it's about being fair and reasonable. He was one of the most generous people I have ever had the pleasure to know. He was truly one in a million!"

"Your dad was an extraordinary person with unlimited positive attributes. Heaven has embraced a beautiful soul."

"I enjoyed those times when I had him to myself in the car. The radio was turned off and no cell phone calls were made. It was purely Kevin time. We talked about stocks, the Boston real estate market and whether it was better for me to buy or lease my next car. I always trusted and followed his wisdom. If the conversation was going well, I would sometimes make a wrong turn and get an extra five minutes in the car of Kevin time."

"We lost a great friend and supporter with the passing of Kevin P. Martin, Sr. on September 10. Kevin—an innovative leader in the field of accounting and founder of our longtime accounting firm, KPM—was involved with the agency from the very beginning. He remained an enthusiastic supporter of our work throughout the years. We are deeply saddened by his loss and will always be grateful for his invaluable guidance and support, as well as his unwavering commitment to helping the most vulnerable people in the Greater Boston community."

"Kevin Sr. was like a second dad to me. After my dad passed, he became my dad. He showed me that I'm a better person than I thought I was."

"He was never too busy and he never complained about being too busy. He never dismissed anything. He led KPM with his heart, his compassion, his problem solving, and, most importantly, his honor. He liked learning and he loved teaching us. His word defined him, and everyone knew it."

"Kevin knew how to be the boss without being bossy."

"Your father was the salt of the earth and such a good person. His generosity and mark on the community will be greatly missed."

"There are only a few people that you will cross in life whose absence diminishes all of us because they are unique and they will not come our way again. Kevin Martin was such a person. Where he saw suffering, he tried to heal it. He made the world a bit brighter with his smile."

"What an accomplished man but no greater accomplishment than his family."

"Your father was a true gentleman, honest, straight-forward, to the point and caring like nobody I have ever met.

"He was larger than life but in a very modest way."

"His commitment to affordable housing has impacted so many more lives than he could ever know."

"He was a gentle, caring soul and I will miss him terribly."

"Smart, gracious, quiet that was Kevin Martin. He always took the time to encourage me and was genuinely interested in the work we do with youth."

"He had a beautiful life and I will be so lucky if I meet him again in Heaven."

"I will remember him as a man of few words, kind and soft-spoken but his voice will continue to be heard through all of you."

"I always admired your dad and appreciated his friendship and wisdom over the last 38 years. I've never met a kinder, gentler soul."

"He always brought a new way of looking at a situation. He always had another perspective on how a transaction could be looked at."

"I've lived my years. I wish it had been me and not my Kevin. He was like a father figure to me which sounds ridiculous because I am older. He was always there for me and my family and I feel very much alone without his guidance."

"A piece of me died today too."

"Your father radiated a kind heart and supportive attitude that is hard to come by in today's world."

"Your father was special in so many ways. Every year he made sure I got Red Sox/Yankees tickets and he always gave me a good-natured ribbing when they were in town."

"I always appreciated when he walked around the office just to check in with people. It was something that everyone talked about. It was a prime example of tone from the top."

We all lead very different lives. What the preacher says about me will be different than what I said about my father.

But I hope that my life stood for something and had meaning and purpose and soul. And what the preacher says about you will *also* be different.

But the question *still* is, "What will the preacher say?" What impact have you made on those around you? How have you loved? How did you give? How did you hug? How did you forgive even when it felt impossible? How did you put others first? It's a beautiful lesson, knowing that it's *never* too late to change course. It's never too late to rewrite the story, and make sure the preacher has some good material with which to work as you continue your journey.

Giving

"Every one to whom much is given, of him much will be required." (Luke 12:48) We've all heard a variation of this line of wisdom offered to us by St. Luke. And we've all smiled, nodded, and sometimes moved on our way.

We often think about this statement in economic terms—but how about in *other* ways? Have you been given much?

Have you been given the love of a parent? The gift of a child? Do you have time? Faith? The gift of friendship? Food? Do you have a roof over your head? Is there any part of your life that is bountiful?

Of course there is. If you think otherwise, I want to take you for coffee and examine it with you.

It is normal to get caught up in our own lives. We get caught up in our own suffering. And we get caught up shoveling the snow, paying the bills, taking care of the kids, maybe even the grandkids, vacuuming the house, going to doctor's appointments, going food shopping, and the list goes on. Let's face it: just living our everyday lives can be *utterly* exhausting. And, of course, we all experienced pandemic fatigue.

At times, real suffering takes us out of the game for a while. It's hard to do for others while we undergo chemo or take care of a parent with Alzheimer's or a husband with ALS. Some days, we can hardly drag ourselves out of bed. Hopefully, during these harder times, *someone* is giving to you, *someone* is giving back or paying it forward.

And, despite our sometimes exhaustion from daily life, as Martin Luther King Jr. challenged us: "Life's persistent and urgent question is, 'What are you doing for others?'"

My father gave. He shined that light for me at an early age. My *very* strong activism was ignited by a loving father showing the way. He took me to meetings, he introduced me to people, he explained to me why people and things and issues beyond our family mattered.

Sometimes my dad wrote the check, but mostly he engaged. He engaged *fully*. He gave his smarts. He gave his time. He asked questions, challenged the status quo. He marveled and wondered. And often, out of that, came a new building, a better program, a favored outcome, or something different that could be measured in a *new* way.

Faith comes in many different shapes and sizes, and part of faith is faith in action. Even after he was diagnosed with ALS, my dad continued to give. It would be fair for him to be bitter, but he wasn't. It would be fair for him to step back, but he didn't. It would be fair to let ALS get the better of him, but he didn't.

The South Boston Catholic Academy was looking to expand with a $3.8-million addition, due to the explosion of families looking for Catholic education in Southie. Despite being sick, I recall a Summer 2019 meeting that my dad attended that included parish clergy, representatives of the Archdiocese of Boston, local politicians, and City of Boston officials, to discuss zoning and the size and scope of the project. I was told that my dad—though weak—commanded the room, ran the meeting, outlined the vision, and put a pledge on the table. And he did this despite what was going on in his own life.

Giving is part of our legacy. It's part of how we are remembered when we die. It's part of our soul. I recall a well-known Boston librarian who—for over forty years—gave her time and tutored local students in reading. It became part of her, *no* check required.

We educate our children in so many ways. Giving is one of them. Kids naturally start out as helpers. They want to help take care of their little brother or sister, and they want to help set the table for dinner. It's during those first years that we have an opportunity to help them seize that innate spirit of generosity. Whether it's having a fun fishbowl on the kitchen counter for loose change, and making a big deal out of delivering it to a local charity every couple of months, or taking our kids to walk the dogs at the local animal shelter, there are many early ways to bond through giving and to teach our children well.

I want to share with you some of the local Boston nonprofits and charities that have become important to my family. If you would like to give in some way, they would so greatly appreciate it, and I have included links to their websites. But no matter the organization, the lesson is to get out of your own way to a more satisfying and fulfilling life by giving back and doing more.

Here's a tip: if you are giving to any organization for the first time, consider checking them out on one or more of the not-for-profit rating sites, www.charitynavigator.org or www.guidestar.org.

ALS One

ALS One is an incredible partnership of world leaders in ALS research and care who have joined forces to help cut bureaucratic red tape to combat the disease more efficiently and effectively for all. Combining resources from Massachusetts General Hospital (MGH), University of Massachusetts Medical Center, ALS Therapy Institute (ALSA TDI), and Compassionate Care ALS (CCALS), ALS One is dedicated to innovative research, and increasing access to care and research to uncover breakthroughs that will help fuel a cure for ALS. I got to know the ALS One family through participating in the nationally known ASICS Falmouth Road Race and being part of the ALS One charity team. ALS One provides care today, while uniting research for a cure tomorrow. www.alsone.org

The ALS Association

The ALS Association's mission is to discover treatments and a cure for ALS, and to serve, advocate for, and empower people affected by ALS to live their lives to the fullest. Because my father died so quickly after his diagnosis, we never became part of the ALS family. However, their work is integral to helping find a cure. Part of the reason I wrote this book was to create awareness about ALS and to help raise important funds for research to find a cure. And for every book you buy or enlist another to buy, important dollars will be donated to ALS. Please help. www.als.org

Bay Cove Human Services

We've been working with Bay Cove since its founding back in 1974. It was one of KPM's very first clients. Since that time, the agency has grown to be one of the largest non-profits in the Commonwealth of Massachusetts, offering a wide range of treatment programs for people with substance abuse disorders, as well as programs for individuals challenged by intellectual/developmental disabilities, mental illness, aging, and homelessness. Mindful that it was part of our earliest beginnings, my father had a very special affection for Bay Cove, its leadership team, and work. www. baycovehumanservices.org

Boston Children's Chorus

Boston Children's Chorus (BCC), called "Ambassadors of Harmony" by the *Boston Globe*, harnesses the power and joy of music to unite Boston's diverse communities, inspire social inquiry, and bring about change. I was privileged to be on BCC's board of directors for over a decade. By examining how lessons of the past can guide us to a more just future together, BCC cultivates empathy to create a more harmonious world, and in 2013 was awarded the National Arts and Humanities Youth Program Award by First Lady Michelle Obama for its exemplary after-school youth arts program. www.bostonchildrenschorus.org

Boston College High School

Boston College High School (BC High) is a world-class, all-male, independent Jesuit preparatory school. It has been forming leaders across every field and every walk of life for more than 150 years. Starting in seventh grade and continuing throughout high school, BC High students tackle relevant subject matter within an academic environment that celebrates collaboration, creativity, and multidisciplinary thought. BC students emerge as compassionate and caring citizens of the world. It was at BC High that I first considered becoming a priest, and I am a proud graduate of the Class of 1982. In July 2010, Jim Cotter, a beloved BC High teacher, coach, guidance counselor, athletic director, and administrator, whose fifty-year tenure helped to shape the lives of thousands of students, died after a long and public battle with ALS. Coach Cotter was an inspiration not only to the BC High community but to friends and family far and wide. www.bchigh.edu

Boys & Girl Clubs of Boston

Boys & Girl Clubs of Boston (BGCB) has been serving the youth of Boston and Chelsea for over 130 years. BGCB's sites and programs are a beacon of hope and opportunity for young people, providing safe places in which members can learn and grow. From career readiness to music production and everything in between, BGCB's programs continue to evolve; what has remained consistent is the loving dedication of the staff, from aquatics directors to social workers, who serve as important role models. I have been privileged to serve in numerous roles over two decades, from local advisory board chair to trustee. www.bgcb.org

Catholic Community Fund

The Catholic Community Fund (CCF) supports the works of Catholic organizations throughout Greater Boston, addressing the needs of people of all faiths. It enables individuals, families, businesses, and organizations to create charitable endowment funds that provide permanent support for Catholic parishes, schools, and other Catholic faith ministries, to help them meet current and future needs. My father served on the board of CCF for many, many years, and I am humbled that the Archdiocese of Boston asked me to serve and carry on the tradition. www.catholiccommunityfund.org

Gate of Heaven Church

Established in 1863, Gate of Heaven Church is one of the largest Roman Catholic parishes in the Archdiocese of Boston and serves the families of South Boston. It's an urban, multiethnic, socially, culturally, and educationally diverse faith community. My father was a Eucharistic minister and parish council member for decades. He was blessed to receive all his sacraments from Gate of Heaven, including the Rite of Christian Burial. www.gateofheavenstbrigid.org

Gavin Foundation

The Gavin Foundation provides comprehensive adult, youth, and community substance abuse education, prevention, and treatment programs. Established in South Boston in 1963, the agency serves over ten thousand individuals and families each year. The Gavin Foundation recognizes that those affected by drugs and alcohol face special challenges in building their recovery capacity, including building support networks, and defining values that guide life choices. www.gavinfoundation.org

Julie's Family Learning Program

Julie's is a South Boston family support, wellness, and education organization that is committed to the development of strong, stable, and healthy family functioning. Julie's provides services that enable under-resourced, head-of-household mothers, their children, and their adult learners to transform their lives and become healthy, successful members of their communities. www.juliesfamily.org

My Brother's Keeper

My Brother's Keeper is a vibrant, welcoming Christian ministry that delivers furniture and food to families in need. Its mission is "To bring the love and hope of Jesus Christ to those in need." My Brother's Keeper was founded in 1988 by a husband and wife serving families in need from the basement of their home. Today, five thousand volunteers and seventeen employees work together from two modern facilities to make over eighteen thousand deliveries each year. As a Christian ministry, My Brother's Keeper offers a crucifix or some reminder of Christ as a gift at each delivery conveying the assistance comes from God through the organization. www.mybrotherskeeper.org

Rian Immigrant Center

The Rian Immigrant Center (formerly the Irish International Immigrant Center) is Boston's welcome center for immigrants and refugees. It has a vision of a shared society where everyone is welcomed and valued, and all enjoy equal opportunities and protections. I was humbled to be chair of the board before taking a sabbatical when my father got sick. By embracing its Irish traditions of hospitality and social justice, the Center empowers immigrants and refugee families from over 120 different countries every year with a comprehensive range of services. www.riancenter.org

St. Agatha Parish

I joined the St. Agatha Parish family in 2020 and it was like a coming home for me. As one of two permanent deacons assigned to the parish, it was the right parish at the right time in my spiritual journey. Filled with an outpouring of hospitality, St. Agatha Parish in Milton, Massachusetts offers a number of ways to grow in faith and get involved, from Bible study, prayer groups, faith formation programming, and service and outreach to others. St. Agatha is the patroness of Sicily, breast cancer patients, rape victims, and nurses. St. Agatha Parish is a vibrant parish community, rich in spirituality and service. www.stagathaparish.org

South Boston Neighborhood House

The South Boston Neighborhood House (The Ollie) is the oldest continuously operated community-based non-profit in South Boston. The mission of The Ollie is to support family and community life in Southie, something for everyone. As a settlement house, it looks to meet the needs of the entire community and offers programs for every part of the family: infants, children, teens, families, and seniors. My father was chair of the board of The Ollie for over a decade. www.sbnh.org

South Boston Catholic Academy
South Boston Catholic Academy is an urban Catholic school in South Boston. The school embraces excellence in education and the firm belief in the uniqueness of the individual. Inspired by traditions of the Catholic faith, family spirit, and academic excellence, the school is committed to meeting the spiritual, physical, and special needs of individual students with a learning environment that is both stimulating and supportive. My father was on the board of the Academy for many, many years, and I am pleased to have taken his seat, carrying on his commitment to love, faith, and education. www.sbcatholicacademy.org

The Arthritis Foundation
The Arthritis Foundation is boldly pursuing a cure for America's number one cause of disability while championing the fight against arthritis with life-changing resources, science, advocacy, and community connections. My family has close connections to The Arthritis Foundation, and I was privileged to serve as chair of the board for both the Massachusetts and New England chapters. www.arthritis.org

Giving can be a powerful agent of change. Giving time, talent, and treasure—and even ideas—can lift spirits and touch hearts, but more importantly, it can promote fair wages, assist in finding a cure, and lead to a change in public policy. Giving offers people a sense of meaning, purpose, and hope for the future.

The not-for-profit sector was a significant part of the work we did as a company. Through the years, I have been humbled to speak and engage with many individuals and groups that have left me with many cherished memories and have impacted my soul forever. From attending an affordable housing ribbon-cutting ceremony to speaking to a group of HIV-positive young men, to attending appreciation night for a group of substance abuse residential treatment program graduates, to getting a tight hug from a youth with Down syndrome at a family forum, to stocking shelves at a food pantry, to giving the opening bullhorn remarks at the starting line for a walk to raise funds for arthritis, they are all beautiful remembrances of trying to make a difference.

Why *don't* people give? I've put a lot of thought into this. My sense is that they don't think that their time or money makes a difference to the outcome. But it does. And they somehow don't buy into the theme of changing the world one something or other at a time. But it can. Every act of kindness *does* make a difference.

When my father got sick, I withdrew from my charity work. I had thought his ALS journey would last years, and I wanted to have as much time with him as possible, so I disengaged from *everything* except work. That's what I needed and wanted to do for him.

I'm not fully back in the game, and, in some ways, I mourn that prior life, too. I feel less in the know and more insular. Giving had always been integral to how I perceived my place in the world, and withdrawing has made me, at times, feel insubstantial and empty. It has been its own journey, getting back in the game.

On one hand, the pandemic insulated us and our volunteer activities. On the other hand, the pandemic allowed us to refocus on both old and new ways of engagement, from checking in on our neighbors, donating blood, sending a dozen pizzas to frontline workers, and alleviating social isolation amongst the elderly and the homebound by making phone calls and writing letters.

Research shows that giving makes us happier. It feels good to give.

Giving changes the world, but it also can change *us* by touching our hearts. Who do you think is happier in life? The givers or the takers? The givers, of course.

All Is Well

"All Is Well."

Those were my dad's final words before he died on Tuesday, September 10, 2019. Intubated and unable to speak, they weren't actual words. They were in the form of his handwritten note in the journal provided to us by MGH. After twenty-four pages of notes, "All Is Well" was the final entry.

I don't now recall the context of the words. Was he asked a question and was answering it, or was he making a statement, or both? I'm not sure.

The good news for him—and for us—is that his final words were not "I'm scared" or "What's going on with me?" or "I'm in pain." There is *so* much anxiety in all those expressions. "All is well" offers a sense of peace, offers an expression of "I'm OK. Don't worry; it will be all right." Maybe it even sounds a bit theatrical, dramatic, or old-fashioned, but no matter. "All is well" is intended to mean that there is nothing to worry about, now.

It means that whatever stress or concern or anxiety that may have existed is no longer present . . . that everything is the way it's supposed to be. It *is* about contentment. The Blessed Mother told him that all would be well again, *and it was.*

As I think about my dad's final words and the way he delivered them, they are, indeed, the sum of the chapters, the sum of his good life well-lived. They are the tattoos of the heart that now grace my right upper arm and my daughter Meghan's left side.

Many of us think that death sets us free. It doesn't. Death doesn't do the work for us. Death takes us from our body but then we still have to walk the rest of the walk. My dad died ready for that walk.

As a kid, despite a tough childhood, my dad was loved by his parents, brothers, and many cousins and aunts and uncles. He grew in wisdom and resilience. He met my mom, and it was nothing short of a beautiful romance. He learned both practicality and how to dream big. He worked hard and built a nationally recognized brand, all while becoming a servant leader. He was quick to forgive, lived a life in the Beatitudes, and had joy in his heart.

There was an Old Testament woman without a name. The Shunammite woman's son died. For no reason, he died. She carried him up, laid him on the bed of Elisha, shut the door, and left. When her husband questioned her, she responded, "It is well. Everything is fine. It is all right." She did not perform heroic acts. She was modest. She offered extreme empathy. She had faith. She offered hope. She was thankful. She stands even today as a testimony of what we can declare no matter what happens. When life's circumstances get the better of us—"All is well." When our faith is challenged—"All is well." When our suffering gets the better of us—"All is well." When the rain falls on our sunny day—"All is well." Is there any circumstance in which we should not be able to say, "All is well?"

And so now, Dad, all is well . . . all is *very* well.

TURNING TO GOD

If you have ALS or another chronic or progressive illness, there's a good chance you've already turned to God. Consider saying a private and personal prayer asking Kevin Martin of South Boston for help. If he can help, he will, because that's what he did on Earth—and why would he stop helping now? It's a simple but good reminder to all of us that death does not separate us and that though our lives may change with death, our lives have not ended. Death does not destroy the bonds that we forge in our lifetimes.

And along the way, if you experience a healing or a miracle or a disease reversal, let me know at kmartinjr@alliswelllessons.com. I, too, would like to know that my dad is still helping as much as he can.

Please pray for my father and for all those whom we love but see no longer . . . and know that my family has you and your family in our prayers.

As I mentioned earlier, my father's family often sang at family parties. We gathered in a circle and the instruments just seemed to come out of nowhere. Dad, this Doris Day song from 1948 is for you.

"Till We Meet Again" by Raymond B. Egan

> *Smile the while you kiss me sad adieu*
> *When the clouds roll by I'll come to you*
> *Then the skies will seem more blue*
> *Down in Lover's Lane, my dearie*
> *Wedding bells will ring so merrily*
> *Every tear will be a memory*
> *So wait and pray each night for me*
> *Till we meet again*
> *Wedding bells will ring so merrily*
> *Every tear will be a memory*
> *So wait and pray each night for me*
> *Till we meet again*

THE LAST WORDS

Much of what is included in this book was referred to in smaller doses in my father's funeral homily, and so I offer you the full text of those sacred words in homage to my father.

My Dear Brothers and Sisters in Christ,

Good morning . . . and thank you.

On behalf of my mother, Claire, and my wife, Lisa, and our kids—Kevin, Connor, Brian, and Meghan—I want to thank you all for coming out this morning to honor my dad. He would be so incredibly touched by this outpouring of love and affection. Thank you . . . Bishop Hennessey, Fr. Casey . . . and to so many of my dear priest and deacon friends for being here today. And thank you to the sixth-grade class of the South Boston Catholic Academy for being here—you are our future, and because of you, that future looks so incredibly bright.

Without a doubt, this moment is surreal. My dad was a super-hero—many of you know that—and he was my superhero . . . *and as crazy as it sounds, I somehow thought that my dad was going to live forever* . . . or at least for a very, very long time.

Now admit it, all of us Google some crazy stuff . . . that moment when we escape from reality—even if just for a few minutes. And so . . . if you Google, "What are the odds . . . " so many unusual things come up . . . things that mostly don't matter . . . but things that are at least engrossing for a few brief moments.

Did you know that:

- The odds of having twins are one out of 250.
- The odds of getting a hole in one is one in 6,000.
- The lifetime odds of being struck by lightning is one in 4,000.
- The odds of being audited by the IRS is one in 200; my dad would want you to know that.
- And . . . the odds of being diagnosed with ALS is about two to three out of 100,000. It's a very rare disease.

You know, I can remember watching TV one night with my dad . . . at my house . . . and we were in that very, very stressful time period waiting for a formal diagnosis . . . and someone had just won the Megabucks and they showed the winner and her family jumping around in disbelief, and my dad turned to me and said, "See, people win different types of lotteries every day . . . we just never think it's going to be us."

I don't want to spend too much time telling you about how my dad died. I want to tell you about how my dad lived and about some of the things he taught our family. But I did want you to know that my dad died from ALS, a chronic and progressive disease—and a reminder to all of us that we never think we are going to be some type of lottery winner—but wouldn't it be simply wonderful if we all lived our lives in that beautiful, hopeful, and joyful way . . . as if we had?

And so, as the odds would also have it, my family also won the lottery . . . with an amazing dad, husband, grandfather, and father-in-law. And so many of you won the lottery with a beautiful friend, colleague, confidante, trusted advisor, mentor, and in some cases, benefactor. Over the last few days, countless people have told me, "Kev, your dad was one in a million."

My mom and dad have been best friends since they were thirteen years old. My mom sits here devastated today. They were inseparable—they went everywhere together—they would sometimes sneak out of work to go to the movies, they went food shopping together . . . and all the junk food that my dad would pick out in aisle eight, my mom would put back on random shelves in aisle nine because she looked at it as her job to keep my dad healthy. The reality is, we've all been inseparable . . . many of you know that we worked together, our places on Cape Cod are 200 feet apart from each other, and we vacationed together across the globe. And as my dad told us just days before he died, "We had a good run."

My dad always taught Lisa and me that all you can give your kids is love, faith, and education . . . and that everything else was a bonus. He gave our family "all of that."

My dad taught us about love. My dad was in love . . . and he stayed in love—with my mom, with his family, and with his God. That's why he got up in the morning. He was a family man—and he loved nothing more than when we were all together, watching the Red Sox, playing board games, and having a big dinner discussing religion, sports, movies, or the next trip. He texted or talked to at least one of his grandchildren mostly every day—we were crying a couple of nights ago over the abundance of voicemails that my kids still have from their beloved Papa.

My dad taught us about faith, about the importance of God . . . about how we look at the world differently when we are a believer. So many people have commented to me that my dad had some indescribable quality that made him shine—and that quality was that he was a believer—that he believed in something more, something better, something eternal . . . he was full of hope and awe and wonder . . . and those qualities came across when you engaged with him. He taught us about the meaning of the Eucharist in our lives. We all find God in our own ways, but there is no doubt that I found part of my road to the diaconate because of the faith example that he and my mom set out for me.

And my dad displayed his faith in so many ways. He was a Eucharistic minister, he was on the board of South Boston Catholic Academy, he was on various boards of the Archdiocese of Boston, and he was on the pastoral committee at Gate of Heaven. He went to Regina Cleary every year, to prepare tax returns for some of the retired priests who lived there . . . he was all about service. He was awarded the Cheverus Award by Cardinal Sean, an award for serving God's people over a long period of time, done so in a very quiet, unassuming, and unrecognized fashion. And doesn't that sound just like Kevin Martin? But he mostly displayed his faith through the example he gave to us.

My dad lived and breathed the Beatitudes. And when we live a life in the Beatitudes, that's when we get a glimpse into the heart of God. My dad radiated Christ in his generosity, in his concern for others, in how he showed forgiveness, in the way he took care of those who were hungry and homeless . . . in his empathy for what was going on in the lives of so many, in the way he made you feel that you were the only person in the room when he was talking to you . . . in his ability to mediate and be a peacemaker. And he did all of this in a very gentle and kind-hearted way.

My dad was afraid. He was afraid of the ALS storm track that was hovering over him, and we believe that my dad was shown mercy from God because "Blessed are the merciful, for they shall be shown mercy." Though it wasn't the miracle we prayed for . . . my dad's quiet death was a beautiful miracle filled with family, vignettes of grace and peace in the most ordinary of ways, exactly as my dad would have wanted it.

His last few days on this earth were spent at the MGH ICU, during which time he dispensed insight and wisdom. He was intubated and, mostly, could not speak, and so, he wrote us notes.

They were life lessons. In one of his notes he wrote, "I must suffer more." Because he knew that as much as we try, it is very difficult to travel through this life . . . onto eternal life . . . without some amount of suffering . . . and in that suffering . . . we experience the fullness of Christ. My dad wanted to receive Jesus fully. And, yes, this notion of suffering is a mystery that we will never fully understand. My dad taught us strength in the face of adversity. He taught us how to die with dignity. He taught us there is a time and a place for everything. He reminded us that salami is not good for you. He taught us how to pray more freely and openly because my dad knew that prayer is a powerful thing that brings us closer to God. He taught us that death is part of living. My dad told us that he was working on a series of puzzles, and once he got one figured out . . . that God would give him another and another and when he completed the last one, the gates of Heaven would open for him on Tuesday. Yes, he died on Tuesday. And isn't that what life is all about? Every day, we are working through a series of puzzles, just trying to figure them out so that we can keep moving.

I would like to share a beautiful message with you from my father that comes from His Heavenly Father, a message delivered to all believers.

God loves you. He wants to be part of your life. You, too, won a beautiful lottery. God believes in you, He envelops you, He roots for you no matter how difficult the days might be . . . He cries for you when things are hard. And, yeah, sometimes bad things happen to amazing people . . . and then God is there in that suffering, in the rubble while we try to figure it out. Jesus wants all of us to know that Kevin is working his way to the Kingdom. Kevin's life may have changed, but it has not ended. My dad dies today with the promise of eternity. My family is in tears today out of a profound sense of loss and love for my dad, but we, too, are believers and we know that we shall see him again.

My dad was a simple, practical guy. We all have a way of making life far more complicated and dramatic than it needs to be—my dad never did that. He worked hard, he loved his family, and he loved his God. And he always recognized Jesus disguised as a sick person, as a teen struggling with addiction, as a homeless family, as an unwed mother . . . and he helped. He always helped. He helped because he was a witness to the Gospel of Jesus Christ. My dad's faith and good works now carry him on this leg of his journey. I miss him terribly, but I know that he will live forever and that he presents himself before God not as a stranger but as a faithful disciple.

Just as when we entered church today, when we are leaving church today, listen to the tolling of the bells . . . the tolling that will be heard across South Boston and far, far beyond . . . because today, Dad, the bells toll for thee.

A CALL TO ACTION

"It means your husband has ALS," the doctor responded to my mother in a somewhat apologetic manner.

"What now?" I asked. "Is there medication available?"

"There are currently two drugs we can offer. One is called Ritulek (Riluzole) and the other is called Radicava. Riluzole has been around for a while, and Radicava is new in the last couple of years, and we are seeing some good success with it. It's the first treatment specifically designed for ALS in over twenty years."

"Tell us about them."

"It's not a cure, but Riluzole can extend life by about three months."

"Three months?

"Yes."

"And how about the other one?

"Radicava slows down the loss of physical function. It reduces the oxidative stress in the body."

"Are there any clinical trials available?"

"There are a number of clinical trials going on at the hospital . . . "

"Can we hear about . . . "

" . . . but none that your father would be eligible for."

"What does that mean?"

"Between his age and his breathing function level, there is nothing for which he meets the eligibility requirements."

Here we were, in one of the top hospitals in the world, and besides some drugs that might extend his life by just a season in the calendar, my father was being sent home with *no* hope, and nothing more than a prescription for a machine to help him cough and another machine to help him breathe.

We need to create hope. Hope is how we make it through our days and how we sleep at night. Hope is what pushes us and challenges us to work harder. Hope carries both patients and families. The funding community, ALS researchers, and the FDA need to work together to create hope.

ALS currently has no meaningful treatment options and is 100 percent fatal. The ALS community needs your help in a few different ways.

First, $115 million was raised through the 2014 ALS Ice Bucket Challenge, spurring a massive increase in The ALS Association's capacity to invest in research. With these needed dollars, researchers made scientific advances, and scientific output has substantially increased. If you participated in the Ice Bucket Challenge, you were one of many funders to help bring to market in September 2022 AMX0035, marketed as Relyvrio, the first newly developed treatment approved for ALS in over five years. AMX0035 appears to slow the progression of ALS and extend life for people living with ALS. Many in the medical community consider getting Relyvrio to market one of the biggest medical breakthroughs of 2022. And as exciting as that is, it's still not enough. If you were inspired by my father's story, please consider taking action, becoming an advocate, and making a donation to The ALS Association at www.als.org.

Second, ALS patients and families need to be engaged earlier than they are currently. "No, we have nothing for you" is not an acceptable answer. Research needs to begin with the patient and not in the laboratory. From access to innovative clinical trials, patient engagement is paramount for better patient outcomes.

Third, not only does the FDA need to support and assist sponsors in the clinical development of drugs targeted for the treatment of ALS, but it must act with urgency to fast-track important drugs to market. It needs to minimize placebos and give access to investigational therapies. People living with ALS are willing to tolerate much greater risk on drugs that meet clinical endpoints, and Congress needs to create more opportunities for people living with ALS to access new and emerging treatments.

No trials were available to my dad, and we need to get to a point where everyone with ALS is offered available treatments and can be in a clinical trial. And these treatments need to be covered by insurance, without delay and without a fight. For this to happen, we must develop collaborative centers that are both funded and supported and have available staff for trials, where innovative approaches are used to accelerate therapy development, and where patients and families are helped and have access to the latest medical knowledge and treatments.

We are at an inflection point, where there is available treatment, but affordability is a major concern in a fractured healthcare system where ALS patients are racing against the clock.

There are many trials, but treatment sites don't have enough staff to offer all of them or enroll interested patients fast enough. And not everyone is eligible, which is what happened to my father. And all of this can change, but there is a lot to do.

Why get involved? Some of these issues are bigger than the ALS community. It's about a mindset. It's about education. It's about mobilization. It's about empowerment. It's about non-partisanship. There's an excellent chance you will *not* contract ALS during your lifetime. But how about cancer? Leukemia? MS? Congestive heart failure? Some other serious illness?

Let me offer you a *dramatic* prose poem—an argument against apathy—to illustrate the point. German Lutheran pastor and theologian Martin Niemöller wrote about the Holocaust:

> First they came for the Communists, and I did not speak out because I was not a Communist.
>
> Then they came for the Socialists, and I did not speak out because I was not a Socialist.
>
> Then they came for the trade unionists, and I did not speak out because I was not a trade unionist.
>
> Then they came for the Jews, and I did not speak out because I was not a Jew.
>
> Then they came for me, and there was no one left to speak out for me.

Will you help us by speaking out? Will you help us in making a difference? Will you join us in delivering hope to get to the place where all is well?

ACKNOWLEDGMENTS

Of course, there are many to thank. To my dad, who gave me the most perfect memories. To my mom, who nurtured me and loved me like no other. You made Dad's life complete. You make our life complete. To my wife, Lisa, where have the years gone? We've made a big, beautiful life together. Thank you for taking care of my dad in a way that only you could. To my kids, Kevin, Connor, Brian, and Meghan, Papa loved you so very much, and you brought him his greatest joy. His eyes lit up every time he saw you or heard your voices. I want to keep Papa's memory alive in you and your children, and that is what inspired this book. To John and Colin, you always lifted us up. To Dr. Mark Hodgeman, my dad appreciated your friendship and a lifetime of good care. To the MGH ICU doctors and nurses, thank you for taking care of us on the most difficult of days. You were kind, compassionate, and caring. To my in-laws, Pete and Carol Carbone, you gave me the greatest gift of your daughter. To Fr. Robert Casey, you guys made a great team. To Fr. Robert Kickham, my father so appreciated your longtime friendship. To Cardinal Sean O'Malley, thank you for visiting my dad in the hospital. You made it OK for him to continue the journey. To the South Boston community, you loved my dad, and he loved you back. To my many family members and friends from Southie, Dorchester, Milton, Canton, Needham, Woburn, Braintree, Quincy, Wilmington, Houston, Cape Cod, New York, Texas, Connecticut, Ireland, and beyond, you called and called and kept inviting us—thank you—you let me do most of the talking, and I apologize. To Ken Davin, Brian Martin, Chad Robinson, Karen Kent, and Chris Pulick, my dad so enjoyed taking the ride with you. To Larry Litwak, longtime family friend, mensch, and company attorney, thank you for forty-five years of good advice. To Fr. Arthur Wright, you have provided me my own glimpse into the heart of God. To Cecelia and Edward Sheehy—may you both rest in peace—you took my dad and his brothers in and made them part of your family. I got the benefit of the love that you gave to him. To Paul and Ed Sheehy, my dad may need a new set of clubs, thank you for always keeping an eye on him. To my dad's brothers—Tom, Jerry, and Mike—I know my dad has wanted to go out for *suppah* with you for quite a while—take him. To the Boston permanent diaconate class of 2013, you are my spiritual brothers from whom I have learned so much about my faith. To my editor, Rob Foreman, you took the time to learn my dad's story and pull parts of it out of me. To the hundreds of former KPM team members and clients, cousins, aunts, and uncles, my dad loved *every* conversation, and he enjoyed unraveling life's puzzles with you. To the staff and parishioners of St. Mary of the Hill's Parish in Milton, Massachusetts, you taught me about faith when I thought I was losing mine. To Fr. Bill Palardy, and all the St. A's team, you welcomed me into St. Agatha Parish at the *exact* right time in my journey. To my team at CohnReznick, you taught me that the best is yet to come. To Morrie Schwartz, take my dad to lunch and show him the ropes. Remember, he doesn't know how to ride a bike. To The ALS Association and ALS researchers, thank you for your care, compassion, and hard work in finding a cure.

ABOUT THE AUTHOR

Kevin P. Martin, Jr. is a partner in a national CPA and consulting firm headquartered in New York. He was ordained a permanent Catholic Deacon in 2013. He lives in Milton, Massachusetts, with his wife, Lisa, and their four children—Kevin, Connor, Brian, and Meghan—and two dogs, Zack and Chloe. He spends a lot of time with his loving mother, Claire, and works to honor his father's legacy every day.